Wake Technical Community College
9101 Fayetteville Road
Raleigh, North Carolina 27603

AMERICAN ★ HISTORY

The AMERICAN REVOLUTION
Fighting for Independence

By Amy B. Rogers

Portions of this book originally appeared in
The American Revolution by John Davenport.

Published in 2017 by
Lucent Press, an Imprint of Greenhaven Publishing, LLC
353 3rd Avenue
Suite 255
New York, NY 10010

Copyright © 2017 Greenhaven Press, a part of Gale, Cengage Learning
Gale and Greenhaven Press are registered trademarks used herein under license.

All new materials copyright © 2017 Lucent Press, an Imprint of Greenhaven Publishing, LLC.

All rights reserved. No part of this book may be reproduced in any form without permission in writing from the publisher, except by a reviewer.

Designer: Deanna Paternostro
Editor: Katie Kawa

Library of Congress Cataloging-in-Publication Data

Names: Rogers, Amy B., author.
Title: The American Revolution : fighting for independence / Amy B. Rogers, John Davenport.
Description: New York : Lucent Press, 2017. | Series: American history | Includes bibliographical references and index.
Identifiers: LCCN 2016036215 (print) | LCCN 2016038624 (ebook) | ISBN 9781534560413 (library bound) | ISBN 9781534560420 (E-book)
Subjects: LCSH: United States--History--Revolution, 1775-1783--Juvenile literature.
Classification: LCC E208 .R635 2017 (print) | LCC E208 (ebook) | DDC 973.3--dc23
LC record available at https://lccn.loc.gov/2016036215

Printed in the United States of America

CPSIA compliance information: Batch #CW17KL: For further information contact Greenhaven Publishing LLC, New York, New York at 1-844-317-7404.

Please visit our website, www.greenhavenpublishing.com. For a free color catalog of all our high-quality books, call toll free 1-844-317-7404 or fax 1-844-317-7405.

Contents

Foreword	4
Setting the Scene: A Timeline	6
Introduction: A Growing Divide	8
Chapter One: Tightening Control	13
Chapter Two: Taxes and Bloodshed	24
Chapter Three: From Boston Harbor to Lexington and Concord	36
Chapter Four: A War for Independence	48
Chapter Five: A Turning Point	61
Chapter Six: War in the South	73
Epilogue: A New Nation	86
Notes	93
For More Information	97
Index	99
Picture Credits	103
About the Author	104

Foreword

The United States is a relatively young country. It has existed as its own nation for more than 200 years, but compared to nations such as China that have existed since ancient times, it is still in its infancy. However, the United States has grown and accomplished much since its birth in 1776. What started as a loose confederation of former British colonies has grown into a major world power whose influence is felt around the globe.

How did the United States manage to develop into a global superpower in such a short time? The answer lies in a close study of its unique history. The story of America is unlike any other—filled with colorful characters, a variety of exciting settings, and events too incredible to be anything other than true.

Too often, the experience of history is lost among the basic facts: names, dates, places, laws, treaties, and battles. These fill countless textbooks, but they are rarely compelling on their own. Far more interesting are the stories that surround those

basic facts. It is in discovering those stories that students are able to see history as a subject filled with life—and a subject that says as much about the present as it does about the past.

The titles in this series allow readers to immerse themselves in the action at pivotal historical moments. They also encourage readers to discuss complex issues in American history—many of which still affect Americans today. These include racism, states' rights, civil liberties, and many other topics that are in the news today but have their roots in the earliest days of America. As such, readers are encouraged to think critically about history and current events.

Each title is filled with excellent tools for research and analysis. Fully cited quotations from historical figures, letters, speeches, and documents provide students with firsthand accounts of major events. Primary sources also bring authority to the text. Sidebars highlight these quotes and primary sources, as well as interesting figures and events. Annotated bibliographies allow students to locate and evaluate sources for further information on the subject.

A deep understanding of America's past is necessary to understand its present and its future. Sometimes you have to look back to see how to best move forward, and that's certainly true when writing the next chapter in the American story.

Setting the Scene:

1756
The Seven Years' War begins.

1760
George III is crowned king of Great Britain.

1762
Catherine the Great becomes the leader of Russia.

1755 — **1758** — **1761** — **1764**

1757
British rule of India begins.

1763
The Seven Years' War ends.

1764
Mozart writes his first symphony.

6 *The American Revolution: Fighting for Independence*

A Timeline

1768
James Cook leaves England on a quest to sail around the world, during which he reaches Australia.

1778
James Cook becomes the first European to reach Hawaii.

| 1767 | 1770 | 1773 | 1776 | 1779 | 1782 | 1785 |

1777
The first American flag is officially adopted by the Continental Congress.

1769
Sir Richard Awkright patents his spinning machine.

1783
The Montgolfier brothers take flight in the first successful hot-air balloon.

Setting the Scene: A Timeline 7

Introduction

A GROWING DIVIDE

The American Revolution did not spring up out of nowhere. Its seeds were sown during years of growing tension between Great Britain and its American colonies. From the establishment of Jamestown in 1607, the relationship between the colonies and Britain was filled with misunderstanding and conflict.

Separated by the vast Atlantic Ocean, the Americans and the British didn't know how to relate to one another. There was too much distance between them, and that distance led to disconnect. Americans believed the British did not share their problems or care about their concerns. Similarly, those living in Britain believed the colonists were acting like ungrateful children who did not respect their leaders, especially the British king.

The divide between the colonists and the British continued to grow more pronounced each year. A distinct lack of trust was present on both sides. Eventually, this division turned violent, and the American Revolution began. The colonies banded together to create an independent nation: the United States of America. They fought to secure that independence and eventually emerged victorious. This war for freedom changed not just America, but the entire world. The ripple effects of the American Revolution and the tensions that led to it can still be felt around the globe today.

Commercial Conflict

The first sign of dangerous division between Britain and its American colonies appeared in the area of trade. Economics has always taken center stage in transatlantic relations between America and Britain. The earliest English settlements, in fact, had been set up explicitly to promote trade. As one 16th-century promoter of colonization said to Queen Elizabeth I, in America "her Majesty and

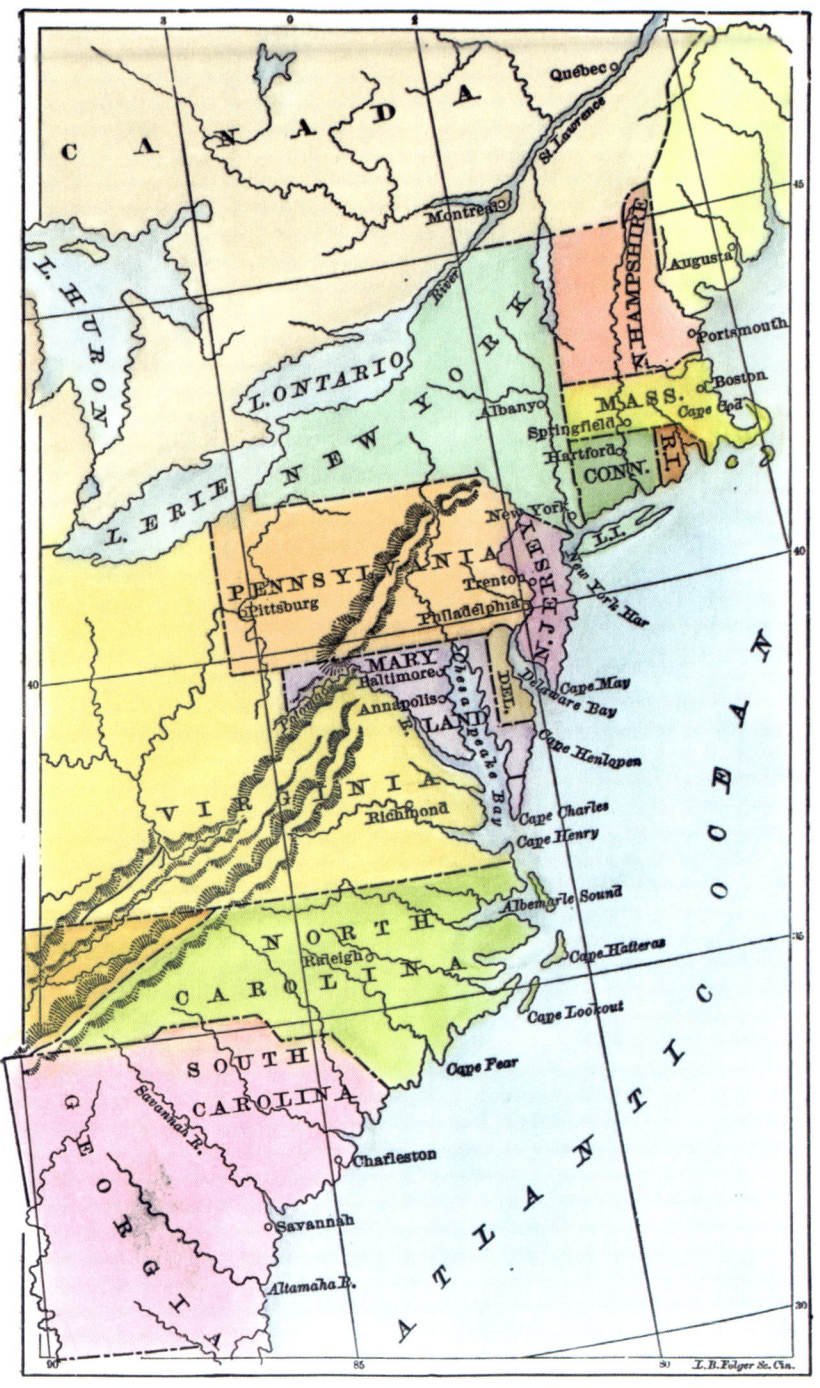

Shown here are the 13 British colonies that came together to create the United States of America.

A Growing Divide 9

her subjects may both enjoy the treasures of mines of silver and gold and the whole trade … filling Her Majesty's coffers to the full."[1] England needed the raw materials and potential markets that only colonies could provide. The resulting settlements produced timber, molasses, grain, hides, and other products of the land offered in abundance by America. Commercial connections between the colonies and the homeland, supplemented later by intercolonial trade, met the needs of both partners. It also turned a handsome profit for each.

This cooperative arrangement flourished for a time, but beginning in the 1730s, it showed signs of breaking down. Starting in the middle of the previous century, the British government had been putting restrictions on colonial trade. It realized that, as the modern economic historians John J. McCusker and Russell R. Menard explain, England's "trade, both imports and exports, depended upon the colonists as producers and consumers."[2] Parliament, the British lawmaking body, passed a series of Navigation Acts starting in 1651. These were commercial laws designed to protect the imperial economy by forcing the colonies to trade only with Britain or other British colonies. In many cases, Americans responded to these laws by ignoring them.

American merchants routinely evaded trade restrictions by smuggling goods in and out of colonial ports. Few American traders felt compelled to obey laws written in faraway London, especially if they lost money by doing so. Worse yet in the eyes of the British, some of the smuggled cargo came from French ports in the West Indies. Considering how often Britain and France were at war, this constituted treason in some Britons' minds. Royal officials often charged Americans with being disloyal as well as dishonest. Trade had become a sore spot in imperial relations. It seemed more than an ocean separated the British and the Americans when it came to commerce.

Political Power

Britain and the colonies disagreed bitterly over trade policies. They clashed no less furiously over the issue of legislative sovereignty. Political leaders in London and their counterparts in the colonial capitals argued about exactly who could write laws for America. The British argued that only Parliament had the power to pass laws applying to British subjects, no matter where they lived. Americans, on the other hand, claimed that no governing body other than local legislatures had the authority to craft and pass legislation for the colonies.

These conflicting claims ultimately led to what the historian Edmund Morgan calls, "a confrontation between the sovereignty of the peoples' representatives in England and the peoples' representatives in the colonies."[3] No state could have two legislative centers of power. Sooner or later, the question of where legislative power was located would have to be answered. Either Parliament or the colonial legislatures would have to be given the final say in very important matters, perhaps the most important being taxation.

Differences on the Battlefield

The contest over legislative authority was a war of words, but real wars were a common occurrence in early America. Bloodshed was something with which colonial Americans were all too familiar. Conflicts between imperial powers—including Britain, France, and Spain—often spread across both Europe and colonies in North America. In most of these conflicts, Britons and Americans marched into battle side by side. Such shared danger and

The British and their Native American allies fought in North America against the French and their Native American allies during the French and Indian War. At the war's end in 1763, Britain became the dominant imperial power in North America.

hardship should have built camaraderie and reinforced a feeling of mutual "Englishness." Instead, colonial warfare bred distrust and disdain, not for the French—often their common enemy—but for each other.

British officers and men who fought in North America considered the colonial militias and provincial armies beside them to be inferior in quality and fighting spirit. The Americans, the British said, lacked soldierly ability and drive. The colonial soldiers were, in short, seen as ill-disciplined amateurs. In the eyes of the British, the Americans were "vagabonds ... the lowest dregs ... on which no dependence could be had ... the scum of the worst people."[4]

The colonial militiamen saw things differently. British officers, they sniffed, were little more than elite snobs who had not earned and did not deserve the right to command troops. When it came to British enlisted men, Americans looked down on them, stating that they were "unacquainted with the American way of war." Ineffective against Native Americans and rumored to engage in criminal behavior, British soldiers were said to be prone to "dastardly behavior [and] deadly panic." Capping off the criticism, American soldiers claimed that they were the only ones who fought for family and community, "not like the regulars, for pay."[5] Both sides underestimated their future opponents.

Holding Off the Inevitable

Conflicts involving the military, politics, trade, and a host of other areas pointed toward a violent rupture in imperial relations. The differences and disagreements between Great Britain and its American colonies grew to proportions that made some sort of conflict inevitable. However, common threats and timely compromises always seemed to hold the empire together. Crises were viewed as family fights within an imperial household that had dangerous enemies just outside the door. Only with the defeat of France in 1763 was the most threatening of those foes removed. After nine years of fighting in North America, Great Britain reigned supreme on the continent. Free from external challenges, Americans and Britons were finally able to settle internal matters once and for all. At this point, though, neither really thought they would do this by turning their muskets away from foreign enemies and toward each other.

Chapter One

TIGHTENING CONTROL

The French and Indian War began in 1754 and eventually spread to Europe in 1756, becoming part of a larger conflict known as the Seven Years' War. When this conflict ended in 1763, it seemed no nation could challenge Britain's claim as the most powerful force in North America. However, the fallout from Britain's victory in the Seven Years' War led to the rise of the group that eventually took that title from the British: the Americans. By trying to hold on to its colonies more tightly after finally defeating France, all Britain managed to do was push them away once and for all.

The Proclamation of 1763

At the time, however, the British saw themselves as the victors in a major struggle. The Treaty of Paris that brought the French and Indian War to a close transferred immense tracts of land to the British. By the treaty's terms, France ceded Canada, Florida, and all the territory between the Appalachian Mountains and the Mississippi River to Great Britain. To keep the peace in this newly won domain, the British parliament drew up the Proclamation of 1763.

Enacted in October of that year, the proclamation declared the British intention to bring peace to "all our loving subjects ... in America."[6] The peace would be ensured by limiting contact between Native Americans and colonists. In fact, a line was drawn on the map of North America that ran along the spine of the Appalachian Mountains. The colonists would stay on one side, the Native Americans on the other. Any settlers already in Native American territory would have "to remove themselves from such settlements"[7] immediately.

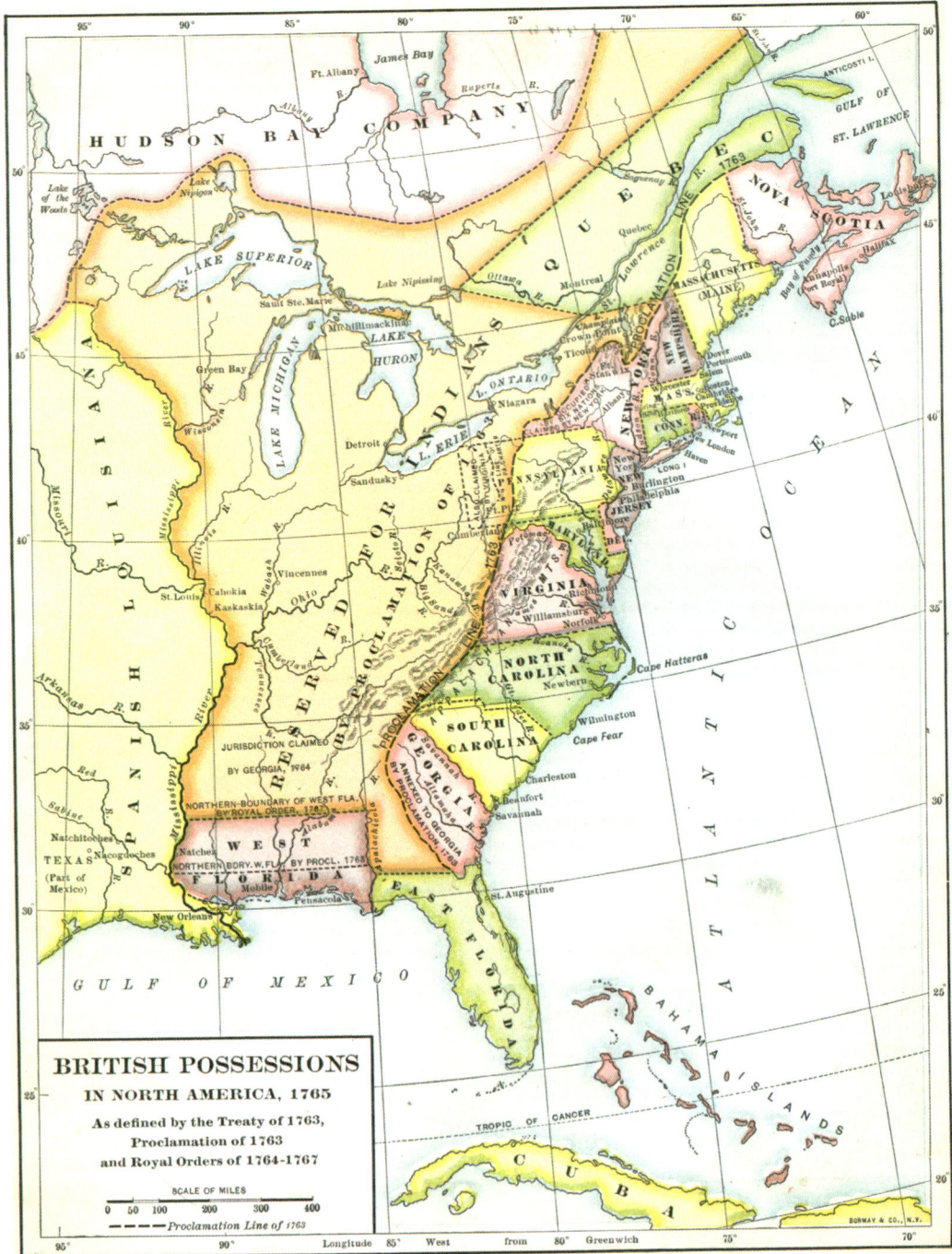

This map shows the line drawn by the Proclamation of 1763. The British claimed this line was a way to keep the peace, but the colonists saw it as a way to stop westward expansion.

14 *The American Revolution: Fighting for Independence*

Problems on the Frontier

The British trusted that the line they drew on a map in London would prevent future conflicts in America. However, by the time news of the Proclamation of 1763 reached America, blood was flowing once again. Angered by British refusal to engage in trade and gift-giving (as the French had done) and further encroachment by colonists on their lands, Native Americans along the frontier rose up. Led by an Ottawa warrior named Pontiac, the Native Americans launched a ferocious assault on American settlements and British forts in May 1763. The colonial response was swift and bloody. Fueled by racism and frustration at Britain's seeming indifference to their plight, frontiersmen attacked Native American villages and camps.

The Americans still saved enough energy to point fingers at the home government. Settlers claimed that the proclamation line protected savage murderers at the expense of westward expansion by the colonists. It also crushed the hopes of colonial farmers who wanted access to western land. The presence of British soldiers along the proclamation line also aroused old fears of tyranny. Royal soldiers, it was claimed, could be used to enforce laws that Americans disagreed with. Americans feared the "redcoats" (British soldiers) might even be part of a scheme to deny the colonists their rights as British subjects. In any case, colonial patience was wearing thin. Americans complained that Parliament seemed to be "in favour of Indians only, against His Majesty's faithful & loyal subjects"[8] east of the disputed line. Colonial suspicions grew.

A Not-So-Sweet Deal

At the height of the war with Pontiac, Parliament did little to ease American fears. In fact, it passed a piece of trade legislation that only made matters worse. The colonists' tempers were rising because of the battles with Native Americans. It was not a good time to begin addressing the debt left over from the war with France. Much of Britain's national debt at the time reflected money spent on either the war or colonial defense. The overall debt was slowing the British economy on its own, but new spending for the military in America was compounding the problem on a monthly basis. In short, Parliament needed to raise money in a hurry.

Taxation was the obvious solution, but imposing new taxes on an already overburdened British middle class would be very unpopular. Taxpayers at home might become more hostile than enemies abroad. An alternative, however, presented itself. Parliament could move to enforce existing trade restrictions and curb smuggling between North America and the West Indies. Smuggling was big business in coastal cities and towns, and one of the most frequently smuggled goods was molasses, despite the passage of an antismuggling law in 1733. The Molasses Act of that year taxed each gallon of molasses imported into America and attempted to limit purchases to those from British suppliers.

Tightening Control

Molasses, Rum, and Slaves

Derived from the sugar grown throughout the Caribbean, molasses, a runny black syrup, was far more prized than sugar itself. When processed by boiling (distillation), molasses yielded rum, the slightly sweet and highly alcoholic beverage that was an important colonial product. Rum was distilled in and exported mainly from New England to other colonies and Great Britain. It was crucial to the so-called "triangular trade" that brought slaves from Africa to the Americas. Along with iron, cloth, and firearms, rum was exchanged for slaves in Africa. The slaves were then sent to the Caribbean to grow sugar, which was transported north to make rum. The rum was eventually traded for more slaves, and the vicious cycle began anew. The booming trade in humans meant that molasses production soared along with it. In 1770, the island of Barbados alone produced more than 1 million gallons (3.8 million L) of molasses that was distilled into more than 2 million gallons (7.6 million L) of rum. The West Indies turned out an astonishing 11 million gallons (42 million L) of molasses, most of which was destined for the rum market. The noted economic historians John J. McCusker and Russell R. Menard have argued that overall economic development in the colonial West Indies "can be largely related to the spread effects not so much of sugar as of molasses and rum."[1] The fact that slavery was so deeply connected to the growth and trade of molasses lends a bitter taste to the history of something so sweet.

1. John J. McCusker and Russell R. Menard, *The Economy of British America, 1607–1789*. Chapel Hill, NC: University of North Carolina Press, 1985, p. 166.

The problem only got worse. Molasses, which is derived from boiled sugar, was the main ingredient in rum. This alcoholic beverage was in high demand in the mid-1700s. It was a valuable commodity and represented a key component in the slave trade that was booming at the time. With many rum distilleries dotting New England, molasses was often in short supply and thus commanded premium prices. Illegally importing molasses, therefore, became the preferred way to lower production costs and maximize profits. As soon as the Molasses Act was passed, colonial traders began smuggling molasses with abandon.

By 1763, rampant smuggling, aided by lax enforcement, was costing the royal treasury huge sums of money each year. Parliament was determined to get this money back. After several government investigations confirmed that the molasses duty, or tax, was essentially uncollected, Parliament passed the Sugar Act of 1764. Followed closely by the Currency Act, which was a law that prohibited the colonies from printing their own money, the Sugar Act took a "carrot and stick" approach to raising revenue. The carrot—or the reward—was a substantial lowering of the molasses duty from six pence to three. It would later be reduced to a mere penny per gallon. The stick—or the punishment—was that the Sugar Act would be strongly enforced. The illegal trade would be choked off by the royal navy, which was granted the authority to seize smugglers' ships and impound them. The owners of these vessels were required to appear not in local court but in a special naval court in Halifax, Nova Scotia, to petition for the return of their property. This part of the Sugar Act was designed to prevent bribery and corruption. When all these things were considered together, it became clear that Parliament intended to collect the money that it felt was rightfully due and use it to offset the cost of defending the colonies.

Would Colonists Care?

Parliament saw nothing in the Sugar Act for Americans to complain about. The evasion of the molasses tax was threatening Britain's economic health. It was also argued that honest, law-abiding citizens had no need to worry; only smugglers and deceitful distillers would be impacted. The colonial elite, particularly New Englanders who benefited from the illegal trade, saw matters differently. They claimed Parliament was exceeding its authority by using the military to enforce trade laws. Colonial leaders, furthermore, accused the home government of concocting a scheme to strangle American trade and hobble a vibrant and growing colonial economy. Samuel Adams, a prominent Boston brewer soon to become America's premier radical, warned ominously that the Sugar Act was only the first step on the road to tyranny. "For if our trade may be taxed," he reasoned, "why not our lands? Why not the produce of our lands and, in short,

Samuel Adams was one of the leading figures of the early revolutionary movement in the colonies.

A Proud Patriot

Samuel Adams's career took him from work as a local brewer to the role of fiery revolutionary and, finally, to public office in the state of Massachusetts. Born in Boston in 1722, one of Adams's first public jobs was as a tax collector. He was known for such lax enforcement that he ended up being fired. He was much more successful in political pursuits, including his time spent serving as a Massachusetts legislator. At the same time, he worked with the Loyal Nine, the organization that evolved into the revolutionary group known as the Sons of Liberty. His exploits over the next five years—including his involvement in organizing what would become known as the Boston Tea Party—put Adams at the forefront of the radical movement against British rule. Between 1770 and 1773, Adams kept the resistance movement alive in Massachusetts, battling all the while with Governor Thomas Hutchinson for influence among a people inching toward open rebellion. Adams became a prominent figure outside of New England in 1774, when he was elected as a delegate to what became known as the First Continental Congress. In 1780, Adams returned to Massachusetts to help write the new state's first constitution. His service in Massachusetts continued after the war. Adams served first as lieutenant governor (1789–1793) and then as governor (1793–1797). After a long and often tumultuous career, Samuel Adams died in 1803.

everything we possess or make use of?"[9]

Clearly exaggerating, Adams hoped that his words would inflame average colonists. He wanted to convince them to rise up and defend the interests of those who profited from molasses smuggling. Unfortunately for Adams and others like him, the Sugar Act did not directly affect most Americans. Only a minority of colonists would experience any real hardship because of this act. Try though they did, the future revolutionary leaders could not rouse the colonist on the street to action—at least not this time.

The Stamp Act

The Sugar Act failed to provoke a huge response that crossed class lines. Those who protested it did so without the support of the masses. Adams and his fellow patriots could not forge a link between their interests and those of their working-class neighbors. Luckily for them, Parliament was about to pass another law that would create just such a connection.

In late 1764, Sir George Grenville,

Shown here is one of the stamps that had to be used on public documents under the Stamp Act.

King George III's prime minister, proposed a special tax for American colonists. The tax was intended to defray the cost of defending the colonies while simultaneously relieving British taxpayers of that burden. The tax would come in the form of royal stamps that Americans would have to buy in order to do business legally. The stamps had to appear on an array of commonplace public documents, including deeds, licenses of various kinds, legal records, clearance papers for ships, newspapers, and even decks of playing cards and dice. If approved by Parliament, Grenville's Stamp Act would go into effect in March 1765.

The proposed bill made perfect sense in England. The stamp tax would reduce the national debt and prod the Americans into paying for their own protection. True, the revenue generated by stamp sales would cover only a percentage of the total amount needed, but a companion piece of legislation, the Quartering Act, would require Americans to cover the costs of supporting troops already stationed in the colonies. Together, the British believed the Stamp and Quartering Acts would ensure that the burden of protecting the empire would be more fairly distributed between British subjects at home and abroad.

The Stamp Act Congress

The Stamp Act's reception in America was far worse than expected. A tax levied only on some of the king's loyal subjects seemed grossly unfair to the colonists. Americans wondered why they should be singled out to pay for maintaining the empire. Unlike the Sugar Act, the new tax impacted every American in one way or another. No matter what one's social status or economic class might be, stamps would have to be purchased.

One by one, colonial legislatures issued formal protests against the Stamp Act. By June 1765, most colonies had made their voices heard. Perhaps the loudest was that of Virginia. There, the House of Burgesses declared that local assemblies had "the only and sole right to lay taxes" on the colonists they represented. Only "the people themselves or … persons chosen by themselves"[10] could determine a proper system of taxation. The famous cry of "no taxation without representation" had been heard for the first time—but certainly not the last.

As the protests spread, colonial leaders began to speak of a united reply to this legislative measure that troubled them all. They pushed for a meeting of a special colonial congress—a Stamp Act Congress—which would answer Parliament in unison. In October 1765, a meeting of the Stamp Act Congress was held in New York City. Delegates representing nine colonies were present. When they finished their work, a set of resolutions lay ready for the king and Parliament to read. In this document, the congress told the king that the Stamp Act "by imposing taxes on the inhabitants of these colonies … [has] a manifest tendency to subvert the rights and liberties of the colonists." The delegates, moreover, stated their belief that "no taxes [should] be imposed on them but with their consent."[11] The point was made: Liberty was based upon the idea of a free people governing—and taxing—themselves.

Violence in Boston

While some colonists talked about their dissatisfaction with British rule, others took more concrete action. Convinced that Parliament was plotting to undermine colonial freedom, Americans began to form loose radical organizations. The most famous and energetic of these

This political cartoon argued Britain could be hurt by alienating the colonies with taxes.

groups began in Boston. Known as the Sons of Liberty, it was a group dedicated to keeping the hated stamps off the streets. The Sons of Liberty directed its most furious attacks against the men who had the job of implementing Parliament's measure—especially Lieutenant Governor Thomas Hutchinson and Andrew Oliver, who was tasked with enforcing the Stamp Act. The lieutenant governor, being a native-born American, suffered being labeled a traitor. As historian Bernard Bailyn writes, "no one in America had been as deliberately and savagely assaulted as Hutchinson [even though] he had opposed the Stamp Act."[12]

The angry words directed at Hutchinson and at the Stamp Act itself soon led to violence. Inflamed by the fierce rhetoric they were hearing, the people of Boston formed a mob on the morning of August 14, 1765. Moving through the quiet streets, the people proceeded to Oliver's house, carrying an effigy—or model—of him. When they arrived, they cut off the mannequin's head, burned its body, and shattered the house's windows. These antics were an unmistakable warning to Oliver.

Less than two weeks later, another mob came dangerously close to open rebellion against British authority. Oliver, having wisely resigned his post, was safe for the time being. This time, the target of the crowd's fury was Hutchinson. In the nighttime darkness of August 26, 1765, Hutchinson's house was demolished just moments after the lieutenant governor and his family fled for their lives. The mob also left with a large sum of money stolen from the home. Hutchinson later complained, "how easy it is for some designing, wicked men to spread false reports, raise suspicions and jealousies in the minds of the populace and enrage them against the innocent."[13] Those "wicked men" referred to the Sons of Liberty, who would soon be seen as the leaders of the push for independence.

Growing Resentment

Boston was only the beginning. By the end of August, rioting had also broken out in Newport, Rhode Island. Radical groups began springing up beyond New England, too. Stamp officers were bullied into quitting their jobs throughout the colonies. The intimidation was so severe that no one wanted to serve as a distributor by the time the Stamp Act was actually enacted in November 1765. In those places where stamps had been taken off ships, they were destroyed by mobs.

When large numbers of colonists began boycotting British goods, trade and the British economy began to suffer. Parliament—its own membership now divided on the issue of American taxation—was unable to control the situation. Francis Bernard, the governor of Massachusetts at the time, summed up matters in America in a letter to the Board of Trade: "The real authority of government is at an end."[14]

Repealing the Stamp Act

News of the turmoil in America soon reached London and the waiting ears of

The Price of Loyalty

Perhaps America's most famous loyalist, Thomas Hutchinson was born in Boston in 1711. His family's Massachusetts roots extended back nearly 100 years. His ancestors included the religious reformer Anne Hutchinson. Hutchinson himself entered public service in 1737. He began as a colonial representative and rose to become lieutenant governor of Massachusetts. Throughout the crisis years of the 1760s and 1770s, Hutchinson's loyalties were torn between his home and his king. He paid dearly for this; Hutchinson was mistrusted by both sides. For three hard and lonely years—from 1771 to 1774—he worked as colonial governor, trying to keep the empire together. His efforts failed, and Hutchinson reluctantly immigrated to England when the American Revolution began. There, he wrote a history of Massachusetts and advised British leaders on American affairs. Hutchinson died in June 1780. His obituary in a Boston newspaper summed up his life by saying that he "was born to be the cause and the victim of popular fury, outrage, and conflagration."[1] Like many other loyalists, Thomas Hutchinson suffered for his devotion to both America and Great Britain.

1. Quoted in Bernard Bailyn, *The Ordeal of Thomas Hutchinson.* Cambridge, MA: Belknap Press of Harvard University Press, 1974, p. 375.

Thomas Hutchinson

a new British prime minister. Displeased with Grenville, George III had replaced him with Charles Watson-Wentworth, Marquis of Rockingham. Rockingham had never been an ardent supporter of the Stamp Act and was well aware of its potential economic and political costs. If he needed any reminding, it was provided by the merchants of London, who formally urged the repeal of the Stamp Act because of its impact on their businesses. Benjamin Franklin—who would become known as a famous Founding Father—also visited Parliament to convince British leaders that Americans took issue not with taxes on imported goods, but with taxes that directly affected colonial commerce, such as those imposed by the Stamp Act.

Rockingham, seeing no other way out, moved to repeal the Stamp Act. He did so, however, with an eye on maintaining Parliament's overall authority. The end product was the Declaratory Act, in which the Stamp Act's repeal was coupled with a clear statement of Parliament's sovereignty. The American colonies, the act read, "have been, are, and of right ought to be subordinate unto, and dependent upon the imperial crown and Parliament of Great Britain … [which could] make laws and statutes … to bind the colonies and people of America … in all cases whatsoever."[15]

On March 4, 1766, after vigorous debate, the House of Commons passed both the repeal and the Declaratory Act. Seven days later, the House of Lords did likewise, and on March 18, King George III gave his approval. The acts covering molasses, currency, and the quartering of troops were left in place—the seeds of future trouble. The British had misjudged the American reaction to the assertion of Parliamentary power. The Sugar and Stamp Acts had produced not only popular resentment and resistance, but also organized radicalism. The Sons of Liberty grew to become an intercolonial model of coordinated action against the British. Americans, thanks to the missteps of British leaders, now possessed the means to oppose efforts to control them, their society, and their destiny. It would not take long before that opposition turned to larger acts of rebellion and, eventually, outright revolution.

Chapter Two

TAXES AND BLOODSHED

The Stamp Act's failure did not convince the British to stop taxing Americans, as many colonists had hoped. In fact, the opposite was true. More than ever, British leaders were convinced that Americans needed to pay for the defense of their lands. The British argued that Americans were still subjects of the British Empire and needed to act as such. Even with an ocean separating them from most of their British brothers and sisters, the British believed that Americans still needed to contribute financially to the empire. With the passage of the Declaratory Act, Parliament made it clear that it still intended to raise revenue by taxing Americans. The question became how it could do so in a way that was more successful than the failed Stamp Act.

The man responsible for finding a new way to get financial contributions from America was Charles Townshend. He served as chancellor of the exchequer, or the financial leader of Britain—much like the secretary of the treasury is in the United States. Townshend believed he could make up for the failure of the Stamp Act and finally get Americans to pay for the growing cost of maintaining peace and stability in the colonies.

Townshend's first order of business was the creation of the Townshend Revenue Act, or the Revenue Act of 1767. The act was described as a way to ensure "a more certain and adequate provision for defraying ... the expenses of defending, protecting, and securing"[16] American lands through the raising of new taxes. The taxes would be levied on goods imported directly from England. These goods included commonly used items, such as lead, paint, paper, glass, and tea.

Townshend also proposed the creation of a group—called the American Board of Customs Commissioners—to combat smuggling in the colonies. Townshend proposed that the members of this group be paid through the new taxes. He also believed the money raised could be used to pay colonial governors and other officials, who were generally paid by the colonies themselves. By doing this, Townshend thought Britain could weaken colonial governments and have more control over what was happening in America.

The Revenue Act was passed in June 1767. The British believed Americans would accept these taxes more easily than they had accepted the Stamp Act because these new taxes affected only imports and not business within the colonies themselves. After Townshend died that year, Lord Frederick North was charged with carrying out this act. North believed so strongly in the Revenue Act that he once told Parliament, "I will never think of repealing it, until I see America prostrate at my feet."[17] This desire to control America—financially and otherwise—grew to define the relationship between the colonies and their mother country in the years to come. With each new assertion

William Knox Speaks Out

Published in 1769, *The Controversy Between Great Britain and her Colonies Reviewed* painstakingly considers each and every colonial claim of British injustice and finds them hollow. Written by William Knox, a former agent for Georgia who worked in London, the pamphlet uses history, law, custom, and economic theory to challenge the colonists' prevailing notions concerning taxation and representation. According to Knox, the colonists' arguments are based on flawed knowledge and a gross misunderstanding of how imperial relationships function. In the pamphlet, Knox claims that if the Americans are correct about the liberties of British subjects, then the connection between them and the parent country are doomed. He goes on to contend that American protests are clear evidence that the colonists and their counterparts in Britain hold totally different ideas about the nature and extent of legitimate power. "What Englishman could desire more of the Colonies than due obedience to that august body, the Parliament of Great Britain?" Knox asks. "But what is due obedience," he continues, "is a matter in which they and the people of England disagree exceedingly." In his eyes, Americans, in fact, define the term as meaning "no obedience at all."[1]

1. William Knox, *The Controversy Between Great Britain and her Colonies Reviewed*. London, UK: J. Almon, 1769; reprint, Boston, MA: Old South Leaflets, p. 7.

of British power, Americans became more resentful. It was a recipe for revolution.

Massachusetts Leads the Way

News of the passage of the Townshend Revenue Act rekindled the flame of resistance that had smoldered in America for more than a year. Once again, Massachusetts took the lead. Meeting in a special session on December 30, 1767, the Massachusetts House of Representatives drafted a letter to be sent to every colony. This letter challenged Parliament's right to tax Americans in any manner, internally or externally. The Revenue Act, the legislators wrote, was an infringement upon their "natural & Constitutional rights … because [Americans] are not represented in the British Parliament … Being separated [from England] by an Ocean of a thousand leagues,"[18] Americans, Massachusetts argued, could only be represented in and taxed by their local assemblies. The Massachusetts representatives had said their piece and now asked to be heard by the other colonies.

Nothing in this letter was entirely new. Indeed, the Pennsylvania lawyer John Dickinson had already called into question the extent of Parliament's authority in his widely read newspaper editorials, which became commonly known as *Letters from a Pennsylvania Farmer*. However, the document drafted by Massachusetts was an official rejection of the power of Parliament. As such, it generated an immediate response from Britain. Most of the colonial assemblies were not in session when the letter arrived. Only three actually responded to it, but those legislatures—New Jersey, Connecticut, and Virginia—agreed with its contents. It seemed unlikely that when the other legislatures convened they would think differently.

The Massachusetts letter expressed a popular opinion and promised to drum up resistance to the Revenue Act. In an effort to stop this from happening, the British government ordered Massachusetts to rescind, or call back, the letter. If the House of Representatives refused, Governor Bernard was authorized to shut down the assembly and send the legislature home. Governors in the other colonies were similarly commanded to dissolve their legislatures if those bodies showed any support for Massachusetts or its letter.

Bernard did as he was told. Rescind or be sent home, he told the legislature. Led by Samuel Adams and James Otis Jr., both prominent members of the Sons of Liberty, the House refused to take back its words on June 30, 1768, and was dissolved. By a margin of 92–17, Massachusetts had rejected the authority of Bernard and Parliament in a single vote. The next day, the *Boston Gazette* published the names of those who voted "no," enshrining them as the "Glorious Ninety-Two."[19] When the governor received a written confirmation of the proceedings, he exclaimed, "Samuel Adams! Every dip of his pen stings like a horned snake."[20]

Fighting for *Liberty*

While the politicians fought it out in the legislature, others in Boston took a more physical approach. John Hancock was familiar in Boston not only as an outspoken radical, but also as a respected and wealthy merchant. His money came from, among other things, trading in wine. It was wine that sat in the cargo hold of Hancock's trade ship *Liberty* when it entered Boston Harbor and unloaded its goods one night in 1768.

Not long after that, the trouble began. The harbor official who had inspected the *Liberty* claimed to have been threatened if he ever revealed that its captain declared less cargo than the ship could hold, which was clear evidence of smuggling. Consequently, customs agents boarded and seized Hancock's sloop while a British warship stood by to protect them.

Noticing that the popular Hancock was having his property confiscated, a crowd gathered on the dock. The crowd became a mob, and soon a riot broke out. The mob attacked the customs agents with clubs. People set fires and smashed windows along the wharf. By the next morning, several buildings were in ruins, and Boston seemed to be on the verge of anarchy. Bernard's response was practical and predictable; the governor asked that troops be sent to restore order. As Lieutenant Governor Hutchinson put it, "government must be aided from without or it must entirely subside and suffer anarchy to rise in its place."[21]

Harboring the same sentiment, Bernard asked General Thomas Gage, who was the commander of British forces in America, for soldiers. Gage quickly approved the request. The general, notifying London of his decision, wrote that "the colonists are taking large strides towards independency." Regulars—British foot soldiers—marching through the streets of Boston, Gage added, would show "that these colonies

John Hancock is best known for being president of the Continental Congress during the time the Declaration of Independence was signed. His signature is the largest on the document.

Taxes and Bloodshed 27

This engraving by Paul Revere shows British ships landing in Boston Harbor in 1768.

are British colonies … and they are not independent states."[22]

Paul Revere, a local silversmith who became famous for his role in the American Revolution, described the late-September arrival of British soldiers. As he stood on the dock, he watched as the warships were tied up and the troops disembarked. Wearing their red-coated uniforms and shiny black boots, the men of the 14th and 29th infantry regiments, who were supported by a detachment of infantry from the 59th and an artillery company, stepped ashore. Revere remarked with disgust on how the soldiers "Formed and Marched with insolent Parade … each soldier having received sixteen rounds of Powder and Ball."[23] The soldiers—armed with gunpowder and musket balls—appeared ready to use deadly force to squash the uprisings in Boston.

Insults and Threats

The Regulars did their best not to provoke the people of Boston. This was a challenge, given the fact that the troops were quartered in the city itself and not at Castle William in Boston Harbor, as was customary. Complicating things further was the relentlessly hostile attitude of the townspeople. Hard looks and insults were commonly flung at the young soldiers, who were ridiculed as "lobsterbacks" because of their red coats. These men had the difficult job of maintaining order in unfriendly territory. Even local public officials took their turn in verbally abusing the royal troops. One Boston judge angrily challenged a group of soldiers he encountered on the street, saying, "Who brought you here? Who sent for you? ... We want none of your guards. We have arms of our own, and can protect ourselves." He ended his tirade with an ominous warning: "You are but a handful. Better take care not to provoke us."[24] It seemed the people of Boston were ready for a fight.

The Bostonians generally despised the soldiers living among them. It did not help that some of the redcoats had dark skin. Many of the drummers and standard bearers for the British regiments were black troops. These men experienced more than the usual amount of taunting and humiliation. Racism as strong as any found in the American South oozed on the streets of Boston. One elderly man felt so much hatred for the black soldiers in the king's service that he could not restrain himself when he passed by a black trooper. "You black rascal!" he exclaimed, "What have you to do with white people's quarrels?"[25] Like so many

The red coats of the "lobsterbacks" stood as a symbol of British tyranny in North America before, during, and after the American Revolution.

Taxes and Bloodshed 29

other black Regulars, this soldier had to let the insult pass without retaliation.

Boycotting British Goods

British troops and the townspeople in Boston eyed one another warily. Neither liked the other very much, and the hostility between them grew. However, in terms of political advantage, the supporters of Parliament's authority certainly had the upper hand. Colonial legislatures had been shut down or frightened into silence. Regular troops preserved law and order. The duties on imports, most significantly the one placed on tea, were still in effect. British rule had been reinvigorated; American hopes had been frustrated. Only one course of action remained open to the colonists as they saw it—meet economic oppression with economic resistance. Drawing on experience gained during the Stamp Act crisis, a call went out from Boston for a boycott of British-made goods. Merchants throughout the colonies were asked to pledge not to import or sell British products until the taxes imposed by the Revenue Act were lifted.

Again, as in 1765, Americans came together in protest. Merchants and manufacturers everywhere banded together in solidarity with their comrades in Boston. Businessmen from Massachusetts to Georgia refused to buy or sell British goods. Taking matters a step further, they announced their intention to shun anyone who did. Those who refused to join the boycott would be considered outcasts. The merchant association of Norwich, Connecticut, for example, openly declared that its members would boycott British goods and "avoid all correspondence with those merchants who shall dare violate these obligations."[26] They wanted nothing to do with people who refused to stand up to the British and their taxes.

The response to the call for a boycott encouraged the Sons of Liberty and other anti-British groups. Virginia planters agreed not to import slaves. Those in North Carolina did likewise. Colonial women and their daughters joined the movement, too. They promised not to serve British tea. Women, who had the primary responsibility for clothing American families, agreed to give up fancy dresses and sew only with "homespun" American cloth. Competing to prove the depth of their convictions, women and girls spun thousands of yards of cloth. Together, Americans hoped to make their voices heard by hitting the British pocketbook.

The Boston Massacre

Parliament could not help but notice the boycott. London traders complained openly about cancelled orders and falling profits. Once more, Parliament was forced to reconsider its decision to tax the Americans. Some prominent politicians quietly urged for the Townshend duties to be repealed, but support for the Revenue Act remained high in many circles. Lord Frederick North—and those who thought as he did—refused to consider lifting the duties. He called for an even

This engraving of the Boston Massacre by Paul Revere reflects the patriot's view of this deadly event rather than the true story.

Taxes and Bloodshed 31

Fighting for Freedom—but Still Not Free

One of the corpses lying in the snow on the night of March 5, 1770, was that of an escaped slave, Crispus Attucks. He is often named one of the first casualties of what would become the American Revolution. Although he was the first black man to die in this conflict, he was certainly not the last. Oppressed and marginalized as they were, many black Americans still actively participated in the American Revolution. An estimated 5,000 black men joined the Continental army, most of them clustered in one of the army's nearly all-black regiments, such as the 1st Rhode Island Regiment. Black soldiers fought alongside the redcoats in even greater numbers. As fighters, regiments such as Lord Dunmore's Ethiopian Regiment were feared by the rebels. The promise of freedom and opportunity drew men to serve in both cases. Unfortunately for these brave men, the war failed to change the status of most. That would have to wait for a far bloodier conflict—the Civil War. Only after that war would all people—including slaves—finally be free throughout America.

tougher reply to colonial stubbornness. "America must fear you," North claimed, "before she can love you … I hope that we shall never think of [repeal]."[27] Many British leaders could think of no good reason to soften the hard line they had taken with the Americans. However, they were about to get one.

British troops had been in Boston for almost two years by the winter of 1770. During that time, local men and soldiers had sometimes fought in the taverns and on the streets. They had thrown horrible insults at one another when their fists were not flying. Young Bostonians and young redcoats had competed aggressively for part-time jobs and full-time relationships with the young women of the town. As the days, weeks, and months passed, the tempers of both parties grew shorter. The threat of violence hung in the frigid Boston air.

Finally, on the evening of March 5, 1770, the mutual hatred boiled over. Alone in front of the Customs House on King Street, a British sentry who was standing guard was confronted by a group of drunken locals. Within minutes, a crowd began to gather. Soon, snowballs and chunks of ice replaced the insults hurled by the mob. Emerging from the guardhouse up the block, Captain Thomas Preston noticed his sentry backed up against the Customs House

32 *The American Revolution: Fighting for Independence*

door, brandishing his bayonet. Preston called out the remainder of the guard to rescue the sentry. In a moment, six soldiers and a corporal marched to the young guard's assistance. When they arrived, they found themselves surrounded by a swelling crowd, yelling and tossing stones as well as snowballs. One of the angry Bostonians called out to Preston, "I hope you do not intend they shall fire upon the inhabitants."[28] To which Preston replied, "By no means, by no means."[29] A short time later, the smell of gun smoke wafted over the street, and dead and wounded citizens lay in the bloody snow. Ultimately, five Americans died in this attack.

Although Paul Revere famously laid the blame on trigger-happy redcoats for the shootings in Boston, no one at the time knew for sure what had happened. The exact details of what came to be called the Boston Massacre were unclear. All anyone could say was that—at some point—a British musket discharged, leading the panicky soldiers to open fire on the citizens who had been tormenting them. It was painfully apparent, though, that whatever the precise cause, the dispute over British authority had reached a dangerous, deadly level.

Hutchinson sensed that matters were spiraling out of control. In the immediate aftermath of the shootings, he had swiftly calmed Boston with the promise of justice through a trial. This trial was held with Samuel Adams's cousin and fellow radical John Adams defending Preston and the soldiers accused of murder. Although Adams opposed British authority, he still supported the rule of law. He did an admirable job arguing the soldiers' case; Preston and all but two of his men were found not guilty. Those two soldiers were convicted of manslaughter, had their thumbs branded with a hot iron, and were released. No one on either side challenged the outcome of the trial. The shock of British soldiers shooting and killing British subjects was too severe. Everyone knew that the dispute over taxes and other legislation had taken a new and potentially explosive turn.

An Uneasy Peace

Even before the Boston Massacre, Parliament searched for a way to halt the growing unrest in the colonies—and the economically damaging boycott of British goods—without appearing to be weak. The Revenue Act had to go, but Parliament's broader authority had to remain absolute. A compromise was reached in April 1770, after a long and serious debate. The Townshend duties would be repealed, with the exception of the duty on tea. This partial repeal satisfied those Britons concerned with saving face and those stunned by the descent into bloodshed. It went into effect immediately.

For the next three years, the uneasy calm was broken only by sporadic acts of defiance, limited almost exclusively to New England. The Sons of Liberty, by and large, went back to their daily lives. Only in Massachusetts did the flame of resistance still burn brightly. There, Hutchinson replaced Bernard as governor, and Samuel Adams labored to hold

Tea from India

Chartered in 1600, the East India Company was established to allow England to compete with France and the Netherlands for control of global trade. Its primary objective was to monopolize the lucrative trade in goods from India, especially spices, silk, cotton, gunpowder components, and tea. Like most English overseas ventures, the East India Company was a private firm that functioned as an extension of the royal government. It was, therefore, a key player in imperial political and economic affairs. The company accumulated so much power in India that it dominated the subcontinent by 1757. By the mid-19th century, it became known for its role in supplying opium to Chinese drug dealers, an activity that had the support of the British government.

Following a disastrous mutiny in 1857, in which Indian soldiers hired by the company rose up in rebellion, the East India Company was dissolved. Its holdings in India were given up to the authorities in London, and by 1873, it was no longer a legal entity. Its short reign of commercial dominance had come to an end.

---

the radical movement together by setting up town committees of correspondence. The committees' job was to keep people informed of government activities.

Here and there, issues popped up that allowed Adams and the radicals to flex their muscles. However, the British were careful to avoid doing anything to cause a resurgence of colonial anger. The radicals, as a result, could sense themselves and their cause slowly becoming irrelevant. Adams and other leaders in the movement needed some new issue to energize the colonists. They desperately needed some point of conflict around which to rally their distracted followers. They found that issue in a cup of tea.

The Tea Act

On May 10, 1773, Parliament passed the Tea Act. Designed to revive the sagging fortunes of the British East India Company, the act ordered that customs duties for this company would "be drawn back and allowed from all teas … [shipped] to any British colonies or plantations in America."[30] Put simply, the East India Company could route its tea shipments through English ports and sell it in America without paying a tax in both places. The British import duty would be paid by the government and Americans would continue to pay their tea tax through the existing duty collected at colonial ports.

Parliament never imagined that the

The Trouble with Tea

People periodically got swept up by fads in the 18th century the same way they do today. One of these fads was tea, which surpassed chocolate and coffee as the English world's drink of choice. Only tobacco proved more popular as a consumer product. Tea was wildly popular in England and America. The tea drunk in the colonies came almost exclusively from British sources such as the East India Company. This combination of fashionable craving and imperial economics meant that disputes involving tea would spill over into a range of other issues. Tea was more than a hot, black, caffeinated drink; it was a symbol of the shared Englishness of people on both sides of the Atlantic. When Britain gave the East India Company a virtual monopoly on the tea trade, it convinced many Americans that Parliament sought to imprison them in a teapot. Americans suddenly viewed a pleasing beverage as a tool of tyranny. This explains the way tea fell out of favor in America during and after the American Revolution.

Americans would rise up in protest against a piece of legislation that did not change their taxes at all. In fact, by lowering the costs to the East India Company, tea sold in America would be less expensive than before. Parliament certainly did not anticipate that it would be accused of trying to tyrannize the colonies. However, that is exactly what happened. The colonists saw the Tea Act as a way to create a monopoly for the East India Company and an unfair tax burden for themselves. Once more, Americans began talking of open resistance.

Chapter Three

FROM BOSTON HARBOR TO LEXINGTON AND CONCORD

Tea played an important role in the rebellious actions that led to the American Revolution. In late 1773, ships carrying tea from the East India Company arrived in several American ports, including New York, Charleston, and Philadelphia. However, three ships that docked in Boston Harbor are the most closely associated with revolutionary action.

The *Dartmouth*, the *Eleanor*, and the *Beaver* arrived in Boston in the fall of 1773. Although their arrival was safe, the same could not be said for what happened later. Citizens of Boston saw these three ships and the tea they carried as symbols of the Tea Act and British oppression. As such, they were huge targets for political radicals. Boston was once again at the center of the political storm, but this time the storm showed no sign of calming down. War was on the horizon, and Massachusetts was set to become its first battleground.

The Boston Tea Party

To protest the Tea Act, colonists in port cities sometimes prevented British ships from unloading their cargo of tea. These ships turned around and went back to England. The Sons of Liberty in Boston tried a similar approach when the *Dartmouth*, the *Eleanor*, and the *Beaver* first appeared in Boston Harbor. They tried to physically stop the men on the ships from bringing the tea onto land.

With the ships docked in the harbor but still loaded with cargo, Samuel Adams and the other radicals went to work. In front of a packed town gathering at the Old South Meeting House, Adams spoke out against the Tea Act and urged his fellow Bostonians to reject Britain's offer of this "shameful luxury." He said to the assembled audience, "We are duty bound to use our most strenuous endeavors to ward off the impending evil, and we are sure that, upon a fair and cool inquiry … you will think this tea now coming to us to be more dreaded than plague." Adams concluded by calling for his listeners to "rise and resist this and every other plan for our destruction."[31] The radical message proved so convincing that the crowd voted almost unanimously to have "the tea ... returned to the place from whence it came, at all events."[32]

Even an appeal directly from the *Dartmouth*'s owner, an American himself, did no good. Francis Rotch traveled to Boston and pleaded with the radicals. The customs collector had informed Rotch that if his ship tried to clear port without unloading its cargo, the royal navy stood by to seize the vessel. Caught in the middle, Rotch begged Adams to let the tea come ashore. Adams stubbornly replied that "the ship must go. The people of Boston and neighboring towns absolutely require and expect it."[33]

Nearly a week later, the stalemate ended in dramatic fashion. On the night of December 16, 1773, a party of men—some disguised as Native Americans—slipped aboard the tea ships. The raid-

News of the Boston Tea Party spread throughout the colonies, and it became a defining moment on the path toward the American Revolution.

From Boston Harbor to Lexington and Concord 37

ers overpowered the crews, opened the holds, and lifted case after case of tea up to the decks. There, with swift ax blows, the chests were chopped apart, and the contents were spilled overboard. Jubilant at the destruction, a young participant in the raid exclaimed, "What a cup of tea we're making for the fishes."[34] Another one of the culprits, when questioned by his wife, told her that he had been out with his friends "making a little saltwater tea."[35] On their way back home through the streets of Boston, the men were treated to the cheers of onlookers. The total amount of damage done that night was impressive: More than 90,000 pounds (40,823 kg) of tea—valued at approximately $1 million in today's currency—had gone into the water.

Britain Responds

The Boston Tea Party marked the end of Parliament's patience with the American colonies, Massachusetts most of all. Furious at the colonists' defiance of its power and the destruction of valuable private property, Parliament decided to crack down. Boston, which was viewed by many Britons as a nest of agitators and traitors, would feel the full effect of the government's might, and all of Massachusetts would be taught a lesson in proper obedience to the king's administration.

With the passage of the Boston Port Act in March 1774, Parliament declared the port of Boston officially closed to all traffic and trade because "dangerous commotions and insurrections have been … raised in the town of Boston."[36] After a three-month grace period, nothing would be permitted to enter or leave the port. The next blow fell in May when the Massachusetts Government Act was passed. The Massachusetts House of Representatives was stripped of its power to appoint colonial officials, including councilors, judges, justices of the peace, and sheriffs. The royal governor—now General Thomas Gage—was tasked with making those appointments. The Boston Port Act and the Massachusetts Government Act were two of what the colonists called the "Intolerable Acts." The other two Intolerable Acts—also called the Coercive Acts—were the Administration of Justice Act and the Quartering Act. The former allowed British officials charged with capital crimes to be sent to Britain for a trial. The latter forced colonists to house British soldiers much like the earlier Quartering Act that had expired in 1770.

When word reached the other colonies about what was going on in Massachusetts, they reacted first with shock and then with anger. Virginia, for instance, set June 1, which was the day the Port Act was scheduled to go into effect, as a day of prayer and support for its "sister colony." The Virginia Assembly asked the colony's people to call upon God to help them avoid "the heavy calamity which threatens destruction to our civil rights, and the evils of civil war."[37] Virginia's royal governor, Lord Dunmore, promptly closed the assembly hall, leaving its delegates with no place to meet

Immigrants' Loyalties

Early on, most immigrants to America came from England, but by the time the American Revolution began, that had changed. Almost 150,000 Scotch-Irish immigrants had reached America by 1760, nearly all of whom settled on the frontier. Also by this same date, 75,000 Germans had arrived, concentrating themselves mainly in farm communities in Pennsylvania and New Jersey. More than 175,000 African slaves were also forced to come to America by this time, living in large number in the South. Between 1760 and 1775, immigration continued: 55,000 Protestants from Ireland, 40,000 settlers from Scotland, and 30,000 people from England crossed the Atlantic to add their numbers to a growing population. These groups went their own ways. The Irish and Scots built their lives on the frontier, while English immigrants settled in cities.

A trend emerged regarding support of the patriots' cause. Newly-arrived immigrants and frontier settlers tended to remain loyal to Britain; those who'd made their homes in cities and on farms over a longer period of time favored revolution. Recent immigrants, it seemed, didn't feel connected to their American neighbors who'd been living in the colonies for a long time. New settlers on the frontier trusted distant British authority more than they trusted the political leaders in the colonies. Slaves' loyalties were determined by their masters' wishes or offers of freedom.

---

except a local tavern. There, they called for another colonial congress—this time a Continental Congress—to address what was now seen as a general assault on American freedom.

The Colonies Unite

Word of the proposed congress spread quickly throughout the colonies. Colonial leaders called for delegations from each colony to meet in Philadelphia, Pennsylvania. By September 5, 1774, 56 men from 12 colonies were ready to discuss what action could be taken to support Massachusetts and protect their own liberties. Only Georgia did not send any representatives to what became known as the First Continental Congress.

To many, the men who met in Philadelphia seemed to be an unimpressive lot. John Adams remarked that it was a shame that America could not produce better leaders. "We have not men fit for the times,"[38] Adams complained.

The First Continental Congress met in Carpenter's Hall in Philadelphia, Pennsylvania, which is shown here. Visitors to this historic city can still visit this building today.

However, an obscure Virginia militia leader spoke up during this meeting and made others take notice. This man earned the attention of his fellow delegates when he offered to "raise one thousand men [and] march myself at their head for the relief of Boston."[39] His name was George Washington.

First Order of Business

The First Continental Congress got down to business without much delay.

40　*The American Revolution: Fighting for Independence*

After some debate, the delegates officially proclaimed that if Parliament did not repeal the Intolerable Acts by December 1, 1774, Americans would begin boycotting British goods. If the Intolerable Acts were not erased by September of the following year, the colonists would no longer export goods, either.

Committees of Inspection were formed to ensure that everyone did as Congress wanted, or else. "Any person," deemed not in compliance with this new Continental Association, it was ordered, "would be universally condemned as the enemies of American liberty." In other words, anyone who chose not to support the radical agenda could expect their one-time friends and neighbors to "break off all dealings with him or her."[40]

Open Rebellion in Massachusetts

The First Continental Congress adjourned in October 1774, agreeing to meet again the following May. Meanwhile, the Massachusetts legislature had illegally come back together after it had been disbanded. It now called itself the Massachusetts Provincial Congress and claimed governing power over the colony. Acting as a legitimate government, the Provincial Congress assumed authority over the Massachusetts militia, reorganized it, and put it under the control of a committee for public safety. This committee then set up special units, known as "minute companies," which were to be ready to fight the British Regulars at a minute's notice. The Massachusetts Provincial Congress also confiscated guns and ammunition from militia stores and authorized the formation of a network of spies to report on British activity inside Boston. One of the leaders of this spy network was Paul Revere.

By December 1774, royal patience had run out. George III declared the colony of Massachusetts to be in a state of rebellion. "Blows must decide," he told Lord Frederick North, "whether they are to be subject to this Country or independent."[41] Accordingly, he authorized Gage to take all necessary measures to restore order in New England. George III, North, and the secretary for American affairs, Lord Dartmouth, all felt Gage was the right man for the job. He was married to an American, he owned land in New York, and he had fought alongside colonial militiamen—including Washington—during the French and Indian War. Gage knew the country and its people. He also did not like Boston. "America is a mere bully," he once remarked, "and the Bostonians are by far the greatest bullies."[42]

Gage planned to deal harshly with these "bullies." He had been given the authority to arrest the leaders of the Massachusetts Provincial Congress as a logical first step in bringing Massachusetts back under British control. The British had a special interest in arresting two men—Samuel Adams and John Hancock—because of their power in Massachusetts. Gage believed he had to plot their arrests carefully. Taking prominent organizers into custody would not be enough. Gage knew he would also have to seize the arms and ammunition belonging to the rebel militias. However, the rumor of royal troops moving against the militias seemed to be enough to incite the colonists to take up arms against the British. As such, Gage was convinced that a cautious approach was the best one.

Secret Messages

After much thinking and planning, General Gage finally moved against the rebellion. Undercover agents had given him the precise location of a large store of weapons in Concord, Massachusetts, that included muskets, ammunition, gunpowder, and even a few cannons. This small town on the banks of a slow-moving river would be his target. The preparations began. At the same time, Gage was hoping to find and arrest Adams and Hancock. He knew they were staying nearby in the town of Lexington, and if he could arrest both men and take back

Paul Revere became famous for his actions in the final hours before the American Revolution officially began. His "midnight ride" has been documented in stories and in artwork, such as this painting, for centuries.

Concord's weapons, it would be a huge blow to the revolutionaries.

Gage's efforts were hardly a secret. Everyone in Boston could sense that something was going on, especially Revere and his network of spies. They watched as British troops in Boston shifted their positions throughout early April 1775. The real question was Gage's route to Concord. Two possible approaches were open to the British. One was straight out of town along the peninsula called the Boston Neck. The other began in Charlestown, Massachusetts, and required crossing a river beforehand. The road chosen by the British would determine the position of the militia used to block them, so it was important to know which one Gage planned to use.

Revere, therefore, decided that as soon as it became certain how the British would get to Concord, a secret message would be sent to the appropriate militia companies. If the Regulars chose to march out along the Neck, one lamp would be hung in the steeple of Boston's Old North Church. If they chose to cross the Charles River before hitting the road to Concord, two lamps would be lit and hung for the rebels to see. Revere volunteered to ride out, under cover of darkness, and alert the rebel leadership while the militia got ready to oppose Gage's force.

The "Midnight Ride"

On the night of Tuesday, April 18, 1775, the British plans were finally revealed. The troops assembled by Gage began loading into boats along the banks of the Charles River. They carried supplies for a few days in the field. Revere had two lamps lifted to the top of the Old North Church and quietly slipped across to Charlestown. From there, he "immediately set off for Lexington, where ... Hancock and Adams were [to tell] them of the movement and it was thought they were the objects."[43] Revere rode hard, dodging British patrols and rousing militiamen along the way. He finally arrived at the Lexington house where Hancock and Adams were staying and demanded to see them. The guard responded by telling Revere to keep down the noise; the rebel leaders were sleeping. "Noise!" Revere yelled, "You'll have noise before long. The Regulars are coming out!"[44] At that, he was allowed to deliver his message. Hancock and Adams made their escape. Then, Revere rode out to alert Concord's defenders.

War Comes to Lexington

As Revere galloped away, Lexington's militia assembled on the village green, prepared to protect the town and block the British column headed for Concord. The British troops were not seeking a fight this early in their mission. Still, being well-trained and well-disciplined men, they would not avoid one if the Americans got in their way at Lexington. By this time, Revere and two riding companions, William Dawes and Samuel Prescott, had been intercepted by British scouts. Dawes and Prescott escaped, but Revere did not. Eventually, the soldiers released him, but not before being told by Revere that the whole countryside had

This statue of a minuteman can be seen today in Lexington. It honors the men who fought in the first battle of the American Revolution.

been alerted to their presence. The British horsemen let Revere go, as he knew they would, and rode hard to inform their commander, Lieutenant Colonel Francis Smith, as well as Major John Pitcairn, who also served as a military leader.

Told that his operation had been discovered, Smith sent word to Boston requesting reinforcements and pushed onward. Around 5:00 a.m., the British arrived in Lexington to find Hancock and Adams gone and Captain John Parker's 77 militiamen waiting for them on the village green. The Regulars neatly formed a skirmish line opposite the Americans, as they had been trained to do. Pitcairn rode forward and ordered the armed townsmen to go home: "Disperse you villains, you rebels! Disperse! Lay down your arms!"[45] At first, the militiamen seemed ready to comply, but then a musket shot cracked the air. No one was sure who fired it, but the Regulars responded as any soldiers would—they opened fire. Within minutes, Lexington Green was cleared of defenders. Eight minutemen died in what became known as the first battle of the American Revolution.

The Return from Concord

The British drums began to beat as the column of soldiers moved out of Lexington. Smith and Pitcairn rode confidently at its head, unaware that Prescott had already warned Concord of their intentions. By the time the Regulars arrived, the militia had reassembled in the hills surrounding the town. Unopposed, the British set about destroying any arms they could find and making a halfhearted effort to find any stray provincial congressmen. They set up defensive positions along the Concord River and secured the North Bridge.

It was at this same North Bridge that the British came under attack for the first time from a sizable American force. Reinforced by minutemen from neighboring towns, the Concord men fought a British scouting party and pushed it backward. At the bridge itself, a confused battle ensued.

The American Revolution: Fighting for Independence

Minutemen

When the Provincial Congress became Massachusetts's revolutionary government in 1774, it necessarily assumed control of and reorganized the colony's militia. The result was a two-tiered military structure that included both regular units and so-called "minute companies." Although imagined today to have implied some sort of elite status, the name had nothing to do with skill level or degree of preparedness. Militias in the 18th century kept their weapons and ammunition in local armories overseen by committees composed of senior militia officers. The colonial governments closely regulated these storage facilities. When trouble arose, militiamen went to their armory, drew their muskets and a prescribed quantity of ammunition, and assembled on the village green. After the alarm had passed, the weapons and ammunition went back into storage. The only difference with minute companies was that their members were allowed to keep their firearms and ammunition at home. This reduced the response time during a crisis.

Neither side really had the advantage or inflicted a great deal of damage on the other. One American recalled of the British marksmen, "their [musket] balls whistled well ... but they fired too high."[46] The militiamen had trouble hitting their targets as well. Nevertheless, Smith thought it best to evacuate Concord and lead his men back to Boston. A relief column had already been dispatched by Gage to meet them along the way.

The minutemen made sure it would not be an easy return trip. The Americans took up positions along the road and peppered Smith's regiment with continuous fire. A British lieutenant remembered how the Regulars were "fired upon from all sides, but mostly from the rear, where people hid in houses till we passed."[47] Another British soldier described how "the Rebels kept up an incessant irregular fire from all points on the column ... they hardly ever fired but under cover of some stone wall, from behind a tree, or out of a house."[48]

Suffering under ferocious musket fire, the British soldiers maintained their order and kept marching. Their officers demonstrated their courage as well. While directing return shots, Pitcairn calmly selected men to sweep out to the sides of the column and clear adjacent houses of rebel snipers. They completed their mission quickly and ruthlessly, using bayonets to

The Battle of Concord, shown here, and the attacks on British soldiers as they returned to Boston proved that the Americans were a force to be reckoned with who would not be put down easily.

silently dispatch their enemies. House by house, stone wall by stone wall, tree by tree, the road to Boston was fought over.

By midday, Smith's regiment had linked up with a relief column led by Brigadier General Hugh Percy. Percy's unit covered Smith's retreat by unleashing cannon fire on the Americans. The minutemen were not trained to face artillery. They broke off the pursuit and fled. The British force withdrew into Boston under the protection of the fortifications Gage had set up. They were safe for the time being but had faced losses. In fact, the British lost more men in these opening battles than the Americans.

Gage praised Smith, Pitcairn, and Percy in his report to London. In his opinion, they "did everything men could do, as did all the officers in general, and the men behaved with their usual intrepidity."[49] There was certainly no shortage of valor and sacrifice on the journey back from Concord. The British soldiers had fought well, but they were also now surrounded by an ever-growing number of militia companies from places throughout New England. Soon, these units were joined by their comrades from other colonies. Drawn by news of the "victory" over the hated "lobsterbacks" and the prospect of fighting against what they believed was a challenge to their liberty, American men gathered around Boston, where fighting had broken out over control of the city. The war had begun. The Massachusetts rebellion now became an American revolution.

46 *The American Revolution: Fighting for Independence*

The Brown Bess

On the eve of the American Revolution, the British army was the best-trained and best-equipped fighting force in the world. No other army had experienced such success on the battlefield; no other army was more respected. The British had many advantages that led to their record of victories—one being raw firepower. For instance, the average British soldier's skill with the popular musket nicknamed the "Brown Bess" proved decisive in battle after battle. Accurate to 75 yards (68.6 m) but able to hit a man-sized target at 100 yards (91.4 m), the "Brown Bess" was lethal in trained hands. During volley fire, the British musket could devastate an enemy. It was a versatile weapon, too, that was faster to reload, easier to maintain, and more durable than other kinds of muskets from this period. When tipped with a blade known as a bayonet, the gun was transformed into a terrifying and deadly close-quarters combat tool. More than one American unit during the war broke and ran at the mere sight of rows of redcoats, their brown muskets sporting gleaming bayonets.

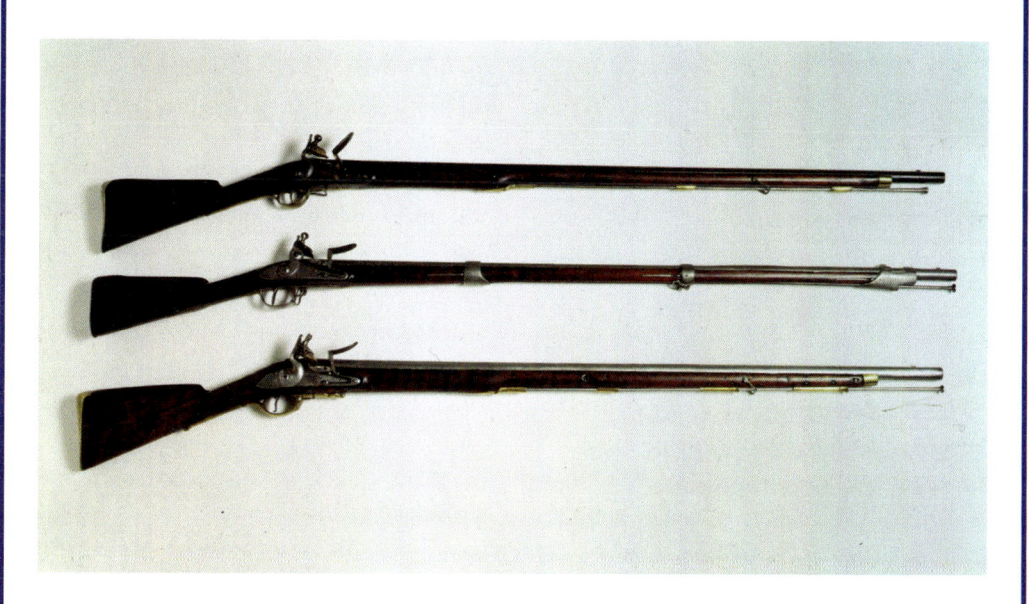

"Brown Bess" muskets

Chapter Four

A WAR FOR INDEPENDENCE

Following the battles at Lexington and Concord, Gage and his troops found themselves trapped within the city limits of Boston. During the spring of 1775, more and more American troops gathered in and around the city. This became known as the Siege of Boston, and it lasted until the next year, when the Americans finally took control of the city that had meant so much to the revolutionary cause.

Long before the siege ended in favor of the Americans, British officials realized Gage could not handle the situation on his own. They sent reinforcements, including Major General Sir William Howe, Major General Sir Henry Clinton, and Major General John Burgoyne. Gage was suspicious of these men and saw them as potential threats to his authority. He feared losing his command position if he did not find a way to control the uprising in Massachusetts. However, he and his fellow British leaders soon discovered that what had once been a conflict largely confined to Massachusetts had grown into a war for independence that united all the colonies against the king.

A United War Effort

While Gage pondered his choices, his opponents formally took action to make the Massachusetts rebellion an intercolonial effort. Reconvening on May 10, 1775, the Second Continental Congress faced an agenda full of important issues. At the top of the list was the fighting in New England. The armed resistance against the British was spreading outward from Boston. Everywhere, people seemed to be picking up muskets to oppose imperial authority. British forts in northern New York had been captured by rebel militiamen, taking the fighting to the Canadian border. In Pennsylvania, rebel sympathizers defied their Quaker colony's reputation for nonviolence and called for the militia to take the field "for the Purpose of defending with Arms, their Property, Liberty, and Lives against all Attempts to deprive them."[50] Three militia battalions, along with cavalry and artillery companies, marched through the streets of Philadelphia itself to show support for their comrades in Massachusetts. Throughout the South, rebel groups prepared to do battle with their loyalist neighbors.

No one at the Second Continental Congress doubted that a revolution was beginning, nor did they have any illusions about the British response. Gage would certainly counterattack, and Parliament had already begun the process of reinforcing the British army in the colonies. Full-scale war was coming, and that required a full-scale American army. To create exactly that kind of organization, Congress officially adopted the military force around Boston, christening it the Continental army. The delegates, to demonstrate colonial unity, authorized the raising of rifle companies in Pennsylvania, Maryland, and Virginia. These troops would move north and make the war a common effort. Shared danger and shared sacrifice would unite Americans. To further stitch the North and South together, George Washington was given command of "all the continental forces, raised, or to be raised, for the defense of American liberty."[51] In doing so, Congress chose a Virginian as the Continental army's commander in chief, which showed that New Englanders were not the only ones contributing to the war effort.

George Washington earned a reputation as a strong leader during his time commanding the Continental army. This reputation made him the perfect choice to serve as the first president of the United States after the American Revolution was over.

Bloodshed on Breed's Hill

Washington quickly began formulating a plan to get the American soldiers into fighting shape. He knew that speed was essential. Washington had to get to Massachusetts and get his new army

A War for Independence **49**

LEXINGTON AND BUNKER HILL

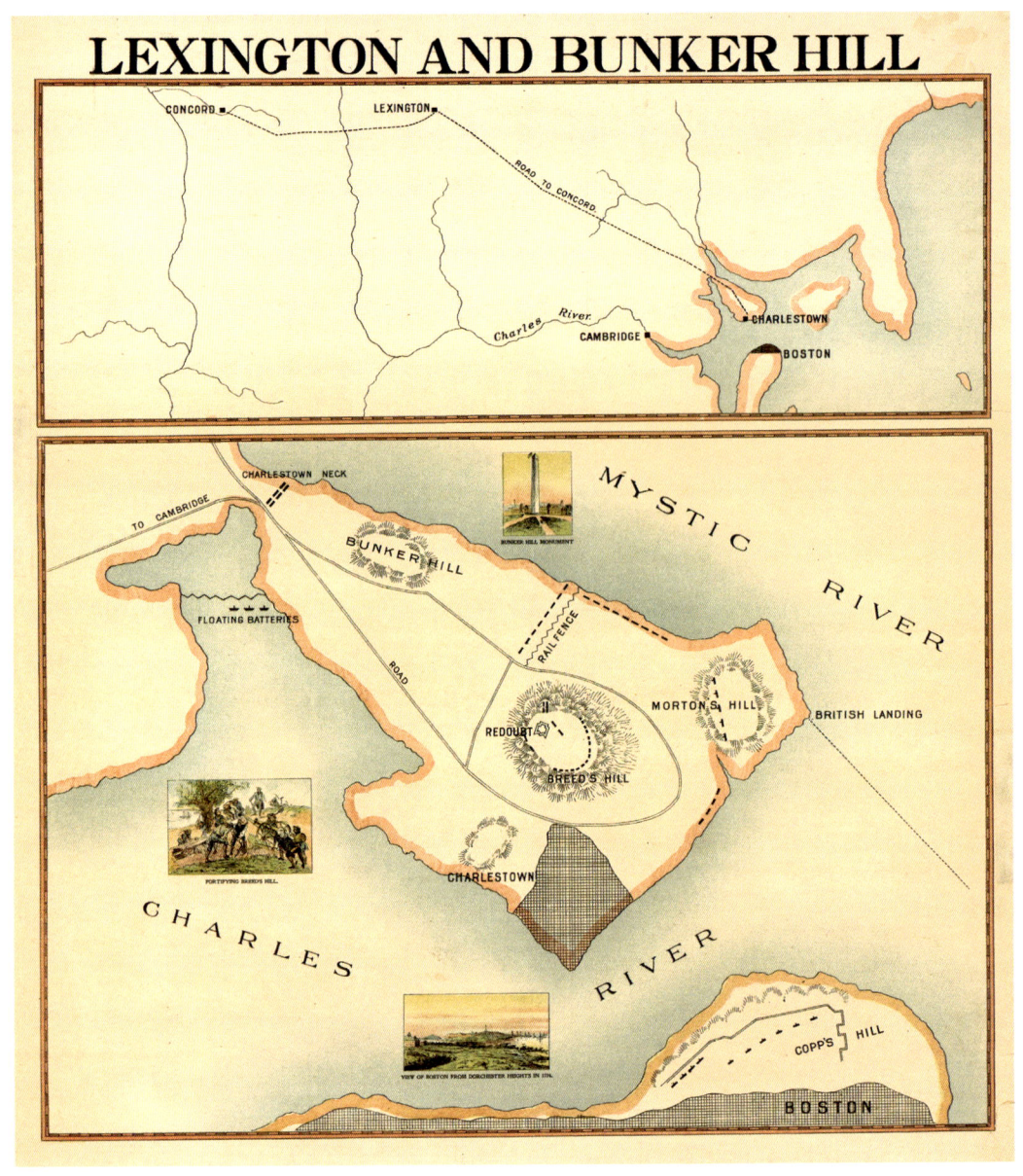

This map shows the locations of Bunker Hill and Breed's Hill. The battle fought here proved that the Americans could inflict heavy causalities upon what was then known as the best army in the world.

ready to do battle against the best military force in the world. More immediately, he had to make sure that the British did not try to break out of Boston. Gage, however, did not wait for him.

Two days after Congress selected

50 *The American Revolution: Fighting for Independence*

Washington to lead the American troops, Gage tried to punch through the siege lines around Boston. After consulting with his new advisers—Howe, Clinton, and Burgoyne—Gage decided to send Howe across the Charles River with troops to smash the Americans, who had entrenched themselves along Breed's Hill. Bunker Hill, which was the initial choice for a defensive line, was decided to be too far from the anticipated landing beach, so the troops dug in on Breed's Hill.

In the early morning hours of June 17, 1775, Howe and a contingent of more than 2,000 men stepped off his boats. Three charges up the hill later, they cleared the Americans off of Breed's Hill, but at a frightful cost. More than 200 British soldiers were dead in the grass; 828 more were wounded, many severely. American losses amounted to 140 dead and 271 wounded.

Clinton, who had never really supported Gage's decision to attack across the Charles River, said later that what became known as the Battle of Bunker Hill was a "dear bought victory, another such would have ruined us."[52] A junior officer serving with Howe's force was a bit more blunt. "The brave men's lives were thrown away," he fumed. "[Gage] as much murdered them as if he had cut their throats himself."[53] Gage, it was said, had won a battle that should not have been fought and taken losses he had not needed to take. Back home in Britain, the general's victory was seen as a defeat. Parliament promptly relieved Gage of command and replaced him with Howe, who would share his responsibilities and authority with Clinton and Burgoyne. Meanwhile, Washington arrived outside of Boston on July 2 to take over operations for the Americans.

The Canadian Campaign

As Washington and his men settled in around Boston, an ambitious and daring scheme took shape in Philadelphia. The Continental Congress decided to try a novel path to victory, one that involved both combat and diplomacy. On July 5, the delegates issued the Olive Branch Petition, asking George III to break off hostilities and start negotiating a settlement that would satisfy the Americans. Simultaneously, Congress authorized an invasion of Canada. The plan was to capture Montreal and Quebec City, bringing the Canadians into a forced union with the rebellious colonies. The Canadian campaign would have two prongs. General Richard Montgomery would take Montreal, while Colonel Benedict Arnold would capture Quebec City after a grueling overland journey through the frozen woods of northern New England. The two prongs would meet at Quebec City, and Canada would then belong to the Continental Congress—or so it was supposed to go.

In actuality, the campaign turned into a disaster. Montgomery took Montreal, and he and Arnold linked up at Quebec City as planned. Arnold's men, however, had been worn down by the march north, and Montgomery was killed soon after his arrival. Arnold himself fell ill and could

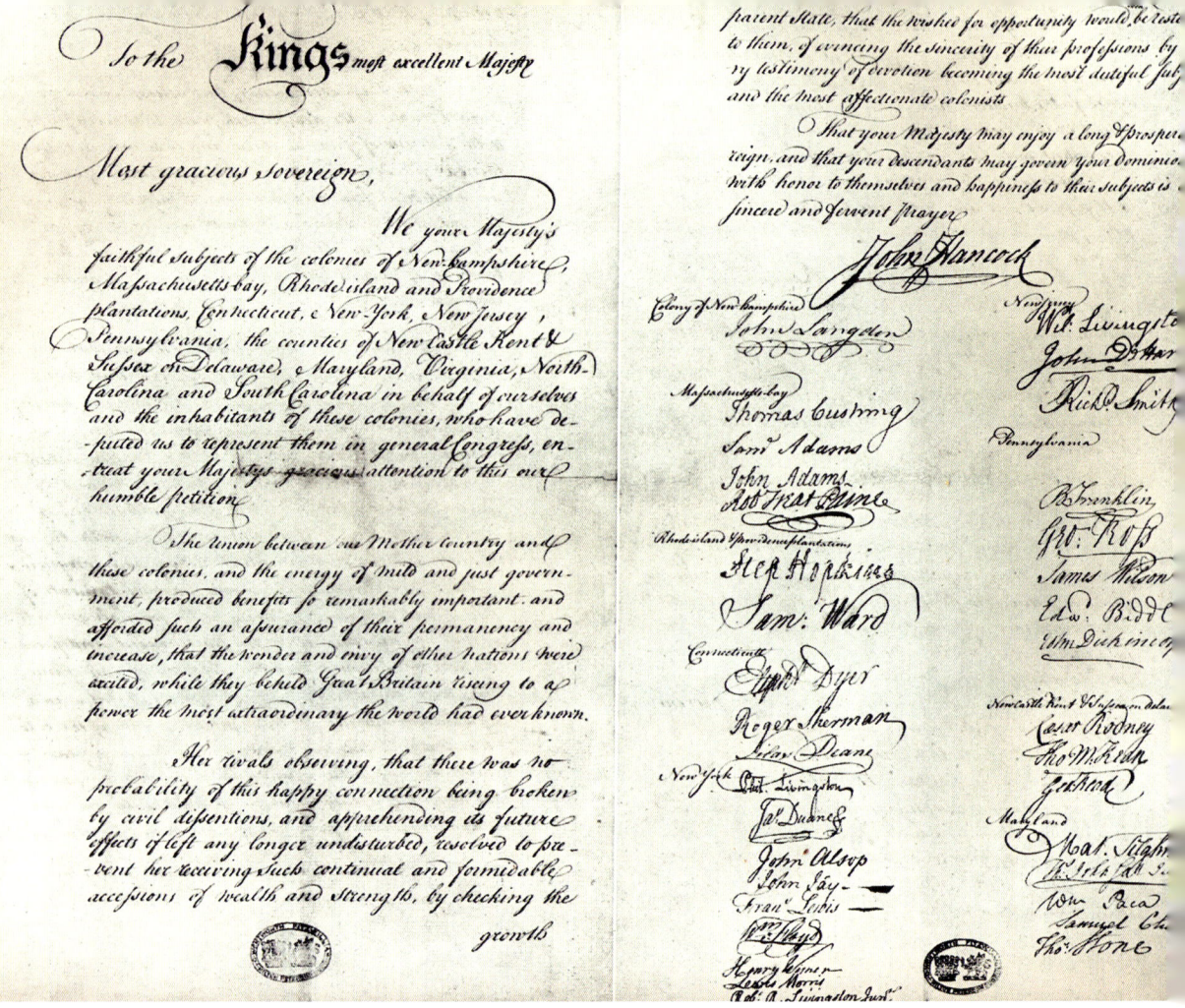

Shown here is a copy of the Olive Branch Petition sent to King George III.

barely direct the assault on the city. Worse still, the local support that had been hoped for failed to materialize. Rather than rising up to aid the rebels from the 13 colonies, Canadians rallied to support the king. Despite boasting that he had "no thought of leaving the proud town, until I first enter it in triumph,"[54] Arnold was compelled to break off the siege of Quebec and retreat to New England. Canada remained solidly British.

"Open and Avowed Rebellion"

As the invasion of Canada was getting underway, Congress received word that George III had refused even to look at the Olive Branch Petition. Instead, he flew into a blind rage at the mere thought of negotiating with men he considered to be criminals. On August 23, 1775, the king formally declared America to be in "an open and avowed Rebellion." He ordered his government "to suppress

52 *The American Revolution: Fighting for Independence*

such Rebellion, and to bring the Traitors to Justice."[55] The Americans were now considered outlaws in the eyes of the British.

Advised of their new status, the delegates in Philadelphia decided to make the most of it. Congress sent agents abroad. Three men in particular were assigned the task of acquiring foreign aid for the rebellion. Arthur Lee, Silas Deane, and Benjamin Franklin were ordered to Paris. Their job was to seek out a sympathetic and well-connected Frenchman willing to convince King Louis XVI to give money and guns to the Americans. Through the services of a playwright named Pierre-Augustin Caron de Beaumarchais, the three agents were introduced to Charles Gravier, comte de Vergennes, who was the chief minister to the French monarch. Vergennes hated the British and saw support for the Americans as a critical first step toward regaining what France had lost in 1763. Secret negotiations began soon afterward.

Highs and Lows

Congress learned of the failure in Quebec around the same time it was informed that Parliament had passed a Prohibitory Act effectively cutting off American trade. Congress also found out that the king had begun hiring German mercenaries for his army in America. The only good news at the time came from Washington.

The siege of Boston forced Howe to evacuate the city. Washington's army acquired cannons from the recently captured British Fort Ticonderoga in New York. With these artillery pieces, the Americans could attack the British troops in Boston from the hills to the south. Howe could not break out, and now he could not stay put. Evacuation was his only option. Packing his belongings, Howe put his men and as many loyal Americans as he could on transport ships. The last one left Boston harbor on March 17, 1776. The cradle of the rebellion fell back into American hands.

The evacuation of Boston considerably lifted spirits in Philadelphia. Howe's departure removed the largest single British force from colonial soil. Even better was the news in May that Louis XVI had authorized the transfer of guns and ammunition to the rebels. France had nursed a grudge against Britain since the Seven Years' War. Aiding the rebellion would hurt the British and possibly lead to a return of some of the territory lost after France's defeat. An agreement with the Americans, therefore, proved too attractive to pass up. The French king allowed Beaumarchais and Vergennes to create a fictitious company, Rodrigue Hortalez et Compagnie, to funnel munitions to the colonies. Cash soon followed. Congress suddenly had two things it desperately needed: money and guns.

French arms proved crucial in the years to come. More than one historian has agreed with writer Robert Harvey's conclusion that "without French arms supplies the American war effort would probably have collapsed in 1776."[56] The twin blows of the king's rejection of peace and the failed Canadian expedition

The Hessians

As the fighting in America expanded in 1775, King George III added to his forces by recruiting German mercenaries, or soldiers who fought for pay alone. Getting these soldiers was easy because the king was technically from the German noble family of Hanover. Being a member of the House of Hanover, he had the ability to hire 30,000 troops from six different German states. A good number came from Hesse-Cassel. Americans, not knowing the exact origins of the Germans, called all of them "Hessians." Some of the mercenaries were used to protect British possessions in Europe, but the majority went to America. There, they fought in several key battles and served as garrison troops in areas securely under British control. German assistance proved useful to the British but ultimately counterproductive. The employment of paid soldiers, who were known for their brutality, turned many potential loyalists against the crown. They were disappointed that their king would send foreign "hirelings," who saw all Americans as the enemy, to settle a dispute between Englishmen. Historians generally feel that using German mercenaries to fight Americans hurt the British cause more than it helped.

---

were softened considerably by Howe's retreat and the French deal. The relief felt by many on the side of the patriots, however, did not last long. A decision was fast approaching that would set the rebellion on the road to total success or complete failure—with no other options in between.

Declaring Independence

During the first winter of the rebellion, in 1775 to 1776, a recently arrived immigrant from England wrote one of the most important political essays in American history. Born in England in 1737, Thomas Paine arrived in the colonies in late 1774. He immediately fell in with a group of radicals who believed that only independence could solve America's problems. Over time, Paine himself came to feel strongly that the colonies would be better off as independent states. He expressed that belief most clearly and convincingly in his January 1776 pamphlet, *Common Sense*.

Common Sense sold more than 100,000 copies in its first year alone. The piece's radical message resonated with a sizable number of American readers. "Government even in its best state," Paine wrote,

Shown here is the Declaration of Independence, which was the document written primarily by Thomas Jefferson to explain the reasons why Americans were forming their own nation. The date this document was adopted—the Fourth of July—is one of the most celebrated days of the year in the United States.

A War for Independence 55

"is but a necessary evil; in its worst state an intolerable one."[57] That, in Paine's opinion, was the current condition of the imperial government—intolerable. Great Britain had become corrupt and vicious. Paine argued that Britain had turned on its own colonies, and "even brutes do not devour their own young, nor savages make war upon their families."[58] Parliament and the king together had committed these sins. Paine concluded, therefore, that the "blood of the slain, the weeping voice of nature cries, 'TIS TIME TO PART."[59] Freedom could now come only from independence.

The process of formally separating from Britain began on May 15, 1776, when Virginia authorized its representatives in Philadelphia to propose independence to the Second Continental Congress. Less than a month later, on June 7, 1776, Virginia's Richard Henry Lee asked his fellow delegates to agree that the colonies "are, and of right ought to be, free and independent states." In recognition of that fact, Lee continued, "all political connection between them and the State of Great Britain is, and ought to be, totally dissolved."[60] Most of the delegates agreed, so Thomas Jefferson, John Adams, Benjamin Franklin, Roger Sherman, and Robert Livingston were directed to write arguably the most revolutionary document the world had ever seen to explain the reasons the colonies were declaring independence. On July 2, Congress held a preliminary vote on independence, and 9 out of the 13 delegations voted for immediate separation.

Although the call for independence was not yet unanimous, John Adams was thrilled by the results of the vote. He wrote to his wife, Abigail, that the "second day of July 1776, will be the most memorable in the history of America."[61] Adams confidently predicted that future generations would celebrate July 2 with festivities and fireworks. As it turned out, he was off by only two days. On July 4, 1776, 12 of the 13 delegations adopted the document known as the Declaration of Independence. This is the date celebrated today as America's birthday. New York was the one state that did not vote on July 4. It adopted the document on July 9. It would be another year before the Articles of Confederation would organize and give legal structure to the new American government, but the deed was done. Now all the young republic had to do was to survive. That would be the hard part.

The Fight for New York City

Since the British evacuation of Boston, Washington had been trying to guess where and when they would return. Anywhere along the coast—from Massachusetts to Georgia—could be the target. The most obvious landing points, however, were near the major port cities, chief among them New York. A landing there would effectively put Howe in control of an important harbor at the mouth of the Hudson River. British control of the Hudson would cut off New England from the rest of America. The British

The Battle of Long Island, shown here, is also known as the Battle of Brooklyn.

could then attack the two parts in turn. Washington, who was aware of all this, moved his growing army to New York. His guess was correct. Howe had indeed decided to retake America through this Hudson River strategy. The general felt certain that victory in New York would mean the end of the rebellion.

In June 1776, Howe's invasion force left Nova Scotia. It consisted of more than 20,000 soldiers, including thousands of German mercenaries. After floating at anchor for a few days off the New Jersey shore, the armada entered New York Harbor and occupied Staten Island on July 3, which was the day before Congress declared independence.

Washington nervously followed the developments. As Howe landed his men, Washington conferred with his staff, which included a highly respected general in the army named Charles Lee. Lee, who was an experienced and aggressive leader, agreed with Washington that the defense of New York City was not possible on the island of Manhattan. The best place to meet Howe would be across the East River on Long Island. That was where Washington wanted to fight.

On August 22, Howe's ships put ashore a strike force of thousands of troops near modern-day Brooklyn, which was southeast of the American front lines. Washington told his army to fight "like men, like soldiers, for all that is worth living for is at stake."[62] His words of encouragement did little good. Soon after the British began their attack on August 27, Washington watched in horror as his line buckled and broke. Surprised by the appearance of British soldiers on their flank, the Americans collapsed. As one of Washington's men recalled, "The main body of the British, by a route we never dreamed of, had surrounded us, and driven within the lines or scattered in the woods, all our men."[63] Washington knew that he could not hold Long Island and could not defend New York City. The only alternative was to fall back, keeping one step ahead of Howe.

The Role of Religion

Religion played a major role in the American Revolution. Ministers, especially those from New England, generated revolutionary fervor before the war and helped maintain it through the toughest times during the fighting. Although some church leaders urged their congregations to remain loyal to Britain, most did not. Americans had long imagined themselves to be on a divine mission to carve a promised land out of the wilderness. The revolution only amplified that sense of purpose. Ministers told their people that the rebel cause was a righteous one, a battle for liberty that had God's approval. This movement was led by Congregationalists, Baptists, Methodists, and Presbyterians, but it also included other denominations. According to historian Edwin S. Gaustad, churches served as "a social, cultural, and political force of unrivalled power"[1] during the American Revolution. It is little wonder that, in the Declaration of Independence, Thomas Jefferson felt compelled to appeal not only to "the opinions of mankind" as he justified the rebellion, but also to "Nature's God."

1. Edwin S. Gaustad, "Religion Before the Revolution," in *The Blackwell Encyclopedia of the American Revolution*, eds. Jack P. Greene and J.R. Pole. Cambridge, MA: Basil Blackwell, 1991, p. 69.

Tough Times

Through sheer luck, a little fog, and the exertions of men from Massachusetts who had experience working boats, Washington withdrew to Manhattan on August 30. He had with him 9,000 tired, beaten men. Howe controlled Long Island, while warships commanded by his brother Admiral Richard Howe ruled the East River. Making a stand on Manhattan would have been disastrous for the American cause. Because of this, Washington kept moving. He evacuated New York and retreated toward New Jersey, narrowly escaping several British attempts to corner him.

Along the way, the casualties and bad news mounted. Each engagement with the British cost Washington dearly in terms of men killed, wounded, and captured. By November, the shrinking Continental army had crossed the Hudson River and was racing south through the sandy pine forests of New Jersey. Behind Washington lay not only the bodies of many of his men but also the ruins of two forts captured by Howe's British and German troops. The American commander had also lost Charles Lee, who was taken prisoner as he slept in a room at a New Jersey tavern.

Washington's army now numbered a mere 3,000 men, and new recruits were becoming scarce. These truly were desperate days, as Thomas Paine, who had joined the army, wrote in his pamphlet, *The American Crisis*, which is sometimes known as *The Crisis*. "These are the times that try men's souls," Paine wrote. "The summer soldier and the sunshine patriot will, in this crisis, shrink from the service of their country."[64] The New Jersey summer had long since turned to fall. The air was cold; snow was not far off. Pursued now by Howe's most able assistant, General Charles Lord Cornwallis, Washington pushed on toward Pennsylvania. The war, it seemed, might end sooner than anyone had imagined.

A Christmas Victory

Howe certainly felt confident that the British would win this war. He was so confident that in addition to hunting down the remnants of Washington's army, he opened peace talks with American representatives. Meeting with John Adams, Benjamin Franklin, and Edward Rutledge in New York, Howe asked them to convey his terms for America's surrender to Congress. The Americans refused. They stated that the British needed to go home and give the colonies their freedom. The brief negotiations ended there, and with them any hope for a diplomatic solution. Matters would be resolved on the battlefield. As historian A.J. Langguth wrote, with the failure of the talks, "the war remained George Washington's to lose or win."[65]

Washington, for his part, was determined not to lose—at least not yet. After crossing the ice-choked Delaware River into Pennsylvania in early December, Washington doubled back. In an assault on December 26, 1776, he attacked the German-manned British outpost at Trenton, New Jersey. The Americans defeated

The famous painting Washington Crossing the Delaware *was painted in 1851 by Emanuel Leutze. This painting depicts the journey Washington and his troops took across the Delaware River to attack the Hessians in the Battle of Trenton.*

the sleepy, drunken Germans, and quickly captured several other small garrisons. Washington even succeeded in stalling the advance of British reinforcements at the Battle of Princeton on January 3, 1777. His men, however, were too worn out and short of vital supplies to go on. Having proven that he still had some fight left in him, Washington took his army into winter quarters at Morristown, New Jersey. Howe decided to spend the winter enjoying the pleasures of New York and left the Americans alone for the time being. The year that had just ended had witnessed the bright hope of independence darkened by military defeat. No one was quite sure what 1777 held in store for the Americans and their revolution.

Chapter Five

A TURNING POINT

Although George Washington and his troops had faced many defeats by the end of 1776, the war was far from over. Howe and his troops had not yet won. As long as the spirit of revolution remained alive in the patriots and Washington continued to lead, there were reasons left to fight.

That thought did not sit well with British leaders. They believed more decisive action needed to be taken to win not just a string of battles against Washington, but the entire war. They created a military strategy that capitalized on Howe's capture of New York City and would end the war with one lethal blow. The goal was to separate New England from southern areas with larger concentrations of loyalists. The British believed this was the best way to put down the rebellion once and for all.

Burgoyne Takes the Lead

After the bloody engagement at Breed's Hill in 1775, London removed Gage from command in America. No one, however, replaced him as commander in chief. In fact, the highest-ranking official in North America was the governor of Canada, Sir Guy Carleton. Howe, Clinton, and Burgoyne effectively shared authority over the British forces.

For all Howe's skill at organizing and commanding armies, he was a timid leader. He was by nature a cautious man, and he was known to harbor some sympathy for the American cause. Like many liberals in Britain, Howe felt that the colonial grievances had some merit to them. Rather than more fighting, the general would have preferred a negotiated settlement and reconciliation. He never lost hope for the possibility of reaching a peaceful settlement with the Americans, who he still saw as his fellow British subjects. In short,

John Burgoyne

Howe was not the best choice to execute a daring plan aimed at conquering New England, which was known as the hotbed of rebellion.

John Burgoyne seemed to be a far better candidate. Burgoyne had arrived in America in June 1775, along with Howe and Clinton. Unlike his colleagues, however, Burgoyne favored an aggressive policy designed to end the rebellion quickly and conclusively. He referred to the actions of the American patriots as "unnatural Rebellion [headed by] the hardened enemies of Great Britain and America."[66] It is not surprising, then, that Burgoyne took the lead in crafting a plan to crush the rebel forces in 1777.

Burgoyne envisioned a three-pronged assault that would cut off New England and deny Washington any hope of coming to its rescue. The main wings of the attacking force would move simultaneously down from Canada and up from New York City along the Hudson River. The third wing would head southward from Canada through the Mohawk Valley in New York. It would eventually join the other two near Albany. Burgoyne would command the element moving south along the Hudson; Howe had the job of pushing upriver from New York City. The Mohawk Valley force would be led by Lieutenant Colonel Barry St. Leger. Burgoyne's soldiers were mainly British and German troops, as well as Canadians, loyalist militiamen, and Iroquois—or Haudenosaunee—allies.

From Philadelphia to Valley Forge

Due to the unwise British command structure in America, Burgoyne could not force Howe to follow his plan. He had to trust that Howe would move up the Hudson River on cue. Burgoyne had no way of knowing that Howe had other ideas. John Adams once remarked that "Howe is a wild General,"[67] meaning that the general was an unpredictable man, and indeed he was. On this occasion in particular, Howe took everyone by surprise by ordering his troops to prepare for battle not up the Hudson but rather more than 100 miles (161 km) to the south in Pennsylvania.

62 *The American Revolution: Fighting for Independence*

Native Americans Choose Sides

During the American Revolution, Native Americans took sides. They chose to throw in their lot with either the British or the colonists. In some cases, they were given incentives for choosing one side or the other. Many allied themselves with the British. A long history of hostility and violence convinced them to fight against their traditional enemies, the colonists. For others, the decision was based on economics. Teaming up with the British would guarantee the continuation of lucrative trading arrangements. Whatever the reason, more than 13,000 Native Americans fought alongside the king's men. The old battle lines between the colonists and Native Americans remained too bold to cross. The colonists despised the Native Americans, so the Native Americans turned to the British for partnership and long-term protection. The Native Americans remembered the proclamation line of 1763 and feared its erasure through American victory. For decades after the war, the image lingered of Britons and Native Americans together attempting to crush the rebellion. The alliance only inflamed preexisting racial hatred and served as an excuse for brutality against Native Americans.

Without consulting Burgoyne, Howe decided to attack Philadelphia, which was the seat of the Continental Congress. He would fulfill his obligation to Burgoyne by sending a token force upriver, but he intended to leave more than 3,000 men in New York City while taking the rest of his command, which numbered more than 10,000 men, to the Chesapeake Bay by sea.

Howe's force reached the outskirts of Philadelphia in early September and met Washington's army at Brandywine Creek. The American general had hurriedly moved his withered Continentals from their winter quarters in New Jersey as soon as he discovered that Howe's immediate objective was the American capital rather than linking up with Burgoyne. On September 11, 1777, the two old foes did battle once again, as they had in 1776. The outcome was the same. The Americans were defeated, and Howe marched his men into Philadelphia just ahead of the now-panicked Congress, which removed itself to the town of Lancaster, Pennsylvania, and then to York.

Washington, who was determined not to give up such a prize as Philadelphia without a better fight, rallied his men for

A Turning Point 63

The American troops who spent the winter with Washington at Valley Forge dealt with freezing conditions and very little food. Many died during this period of sickness and starvation, which was seen as one of the darkest times of the American Revolution.

an attack on the northern edge of the British army. At Germantown, Pennsyl- vania, on October 4, 1777, Washington landed his blow, but the British won again. Dejected after losing two battles and a major American city, Washington took his troops west and settled in at a part of Pennsylvania called Valley Forge. There, they endured a brutal winter that nearly cost Washington his entire army and his job as commander in chief.

The Battle of Saratoga

Burgoyne had no intention of letting Howe's unexpected campaign ruin his effort to win the war. The general had long ago decided to drive on, no matter what the cost. "THIS ARMY MUST NOT RETREAT,"[68] he forcefully stated. With that, Burgoyne plunged southward. Almost from the start, things went wrong. St. Leger's force stalled in the Mohawk Valley and was then turned back by a strong American contingent led by Arnold. The American soldiers were better equipped and better led than Burgoyne had anticipated. The efforts of Franklin to funnel French arms and ammunition to the Continental army had paid off; the American army in northern New York had plenty of both. More troubling for Burgoyne, his counterparts on the American side included not only the very able Arnold, but also the equally formidable General Horatio Gates and Colonel Daniel Morgan. Without Howe's

A Brutal Winter

In the fall of 1777, George Washington took his battered army into winter quarters at Valley Forge, Pennsylvania. Less than 20 miles (32.2 km) away, his opponent, General Howe, rested comfortably in Philadelphia. Howe actually looked forward to a lull in the fighting; Washington prayed simply to endure it. The winter of 1777 to 1778 was a harsh one. Men left camp in a steady stream, unable to cope with the hardships of winter in a military camp. Soldiers lived in tiny huts in groups of 12. Clothing became scarce, leading frequently to frostbite. Sickness and hunger soon followed. Washington did the best he could to withstand the weather and prevent the desertion of his troops. He struggled to get supplies and occupied his men with training exercises and drills led by the Baron von Steuben. All the while, he had to defend himself against the efforts of a small group of officers determined to have him relieved of command. Known to history as the "Conway Cabal," after its leader Thomas Conway, the group lobbied to have Washington replaced by General Horatio Gates. They failed, and Washington held his post. His army survived the winter and went on to victory.

This painting shows Burgoyne's surrender at Saratoga, which was considered a turning point in the American Revolution.

contribution, Burgoyne's army was at a distinct disadvantage in the coming fight.

Still, Burgoyne pushed on. He slammed into the Americans on September 19 at Freeman's Farm in New York, in a battle that is sometimes called the First Battle of Saratoga. Furious fighting ensued, in which the Americans matched

66 *The American Revolution: Fighting for Independence*

their shooting skills against the British expertise with bayonets. An American officer remembered with awe the determination shown by the contesting forces. "Both armies," he wrote, "seemed determined to conquer or die. One continual blaze [of gunfire] without any intermission until dark, when by consent of both parties it ceased."[69] One of Burgoyne's officers recalled that the "crash of cannon and musketry never ceased till darkness parted us."[70] By that time, both sides were exhausted and battered. Although Burgoyne technically won the engagement, his soldiers had been badly bloodied by the fierce American attacks.

Burgoyne tested his enemy again on October 7 in what became known as the Second Battle of Saratoga. This time, the American troops, admirably led by Arnold, forced the British to retreat after a brutal fight at Bemis Heights. One of Britain's best generals was forced to admit that his men had been outfought and

Filling the Ranks

The call to arms in 1775 drew multitudes of citizen-soldiers to the rebel forces. They saw themselves as simple farmers whose virtue would win the day, battling in support of God-given liberty against tyranny. However, the brutal defeats of 1776 sent most of these early rebel recruits scurrying home. Although viewed today as heroes, many militiamen, in fact, proved to be just what Thomas Paine said they were—"summer soldiers" and "sunshine patriots." They shrank from service when America needed them most. Beginning in 1777, a new kind of soldier fought for liberty against the most powerful army in the world. Lured into service by the promise of food, clothing, a $20 bonus, and a guarantee of 100 acres (40.5 ha) of land after the war, thousands of working-class men joined the Continental army. They were white and black, immigrants and men born in America, but they shared a place at the bottom of the social ladder. They had nothing to offer or lose but their lives; they were men the rest of America considered expendable. Historian Charles Royster wrote, "Once a long-term army became necessary, the public decided that it was the duty of only some men ... to fill its ranks."[1] Those "some men" were laborers, mechanics, and slaves. Few monuments to their sacrifices were ever built—despite their bravery and heroism.

1. Charles Royster, *A Revolutionary People at War: The Continental Army and American Character, 1775–1783*. New York, NY: W.W. Norton, 1979, p. 129.

he had been "outgeneraled." Burgoyne and his troops fell back to a position just outside Saratoga, which was where Gates and Arnold surrounded them. Burgoyne and his entire force were left with no escape. The only option was to surrender. Negotiations began on October 16, 1777. The next day, Burgoyne surrendered his sword, 27 artillery pieces, 5,000 muskets, and more than 5,000 troops to Gates. Upon meeting Gates, Burgoyne said calmly, "The fortunes of war, General, have made me your prisoner."[71] One of his generals, however, assessed the defeat in more emotional terms: "Poor General Burgoyne! Oh, fatal ambition!"[72] Burgoyne's officers and men were not allowed to return to England as Gates had promised in the surrender document, which was known as a convention. Only Burgoyne could go home. The rest of his force, which became known as the "Convention Army," was marched to Virginia to sit out the war in relative peace and comfort.

A Global Conflict

The consequences of Burgoyne's defeat at Saratoga became immediately apparent. Washington, trying to keep his demoralized and frostbitten army at Valley Forge from disintegrating, suddenly had one less enemy army to worry about. He could concentrate on resupplying his troops and training them to fight the British Regulars on their own terms. He was aided in this task by invaluable advice and assistance from European officers who had signed on to the rebel cause. Chief among these volunteers were Casimir Pulaski, a Polish cavalryman, and Baron Friedrich Wilhelm von Steuben. Pulaski helped Washington create an effective cavalry corps to support his infantry, while von Steuben was instrumental in

The Marquis de Lafayette, shown here, joined the Continental army when he was only 19 years old. He developed a close relationship with George Washington and became a respected and trusted leader of American troops.

training the Continental army in European battlefield tactics. Neither these men nor Washington himself could make the winter any warmer or food and medicine any more plentiful. Washington's army suffered greatly during that winter of 1777 to 1778. However, the victory at Saratoga did promise to make Washington's job for the rest of 1778 and beyond a bit easier.

Washington was certainly heartened by another consequence of the success at Saratoga: France finally decided to fully and openly support the revolutionary cause. Since the spring of 1776, arms and ammunition had been arriving in America through Rodrigue Hortalez and other smaller operations. These supplies had come almost exclusively from France, and they came in relative abundance. Indeed, Washington could thank covert French aid for keeping his army in the field against the British. Helpful as this was, however, America needed more. America needed the French army and navy. Only the addition of professional French soldiers and powerful French warships could turn the tide of the war. To be sure, a few French volunteers were already holding Continental commands. The most famous was the young French nobleman Marie-Joseph-Paul-Yves-Roch-Gilbert du Motier, Marquis de Lafayette. Soon to distinguish himself during the war's southern campaign, Lafayette had arrived in America in 1777 and had fought alongside Washington at the Battle of Brandywine. Although valued, such support was ultimately insufficient. The French had to come across the Atlantic in greater numbers as part of a formal alliance to make a real difference.

King Louis XVI was reluctant to support the rebellion at first. He demanded clear evidence that the new republic could survive before he committed the power and prestige of France in support. He received the evidence he wanted with the victory at Saratoga. Gates and Arnold had proven that American armies could defeat their British counterparts in open-field battle. As a result, the king made the decision to form an alliance with America and throw the military might of France into the war, effectively turning the American Revolution into a world war. From India to the Caribbean, French and British forces began to clash.

Negotiations began between the French government and the American team led by Franklin, who was now the senior member of the committee that had been in France for almost two years. After long talks, the American and French representatives settled on the precise wording of a Treaty of Amity and Commerce, as well as a Treaty of Alliance. These were signed by both parties on February 6, 1778. These documents formally pledged that France and America now formed a "defensive alliance [that] is to maintain effectually the liberty, sovereignty, and independence of the said United States, as well in matters of government as of commerce."[73] France and America would trade with one another and fight side by side "until the moment of the cessation of the present war between the United States and England."[74] Soon after, French

A Naval Hero

John Paul Jones was America's only naval commander of note during the Revolution, and the battles he fought were the only significant engagements involving the American navy. Born John Paul in Scotland in 1747, he went to sea at the age of 13. As a boy, he learned everything he could about the ships of the day. He later ran into trouble as a young man. He was accused of murder and forced to flee to America, adding the name "Jones" to hide his identity. After joining the American forces, he compiled an impressive record. Jones captured 16 British ships before being dispatched to European waters. There, he raided the English coast and attacked merchant shipping. In September 1779, he was finally cornered by the royal navy off Flamborough Head, England. Jones, commanding the *Bonhomme Richard*, faced off against a number of British vessels, the most dangerous being the *Serapis*. What followed was a classic 18th-century sea battle. Locked together by grappling hooks, the *Bonhomme Richard* and the *Serapis* pounded away at one another. After a ferocious fight, the *Serapis* surrendered. Jones's victory was celebrated throughout America and is counted as the American navy's first triumph. John Paul Jones died quietly in France in 1792.

John Paul Jones

soldiers boarded ships, preparing to sail for war against the British in America once again.

Clinton's New Plan

The disaster at Saratoga and news of the French-American treaty forced Parliament to take action. Blamed for everything that had happened in 1777, Howe was relieved of his command and replaced by Clinton.

If Clinton hoped to inherit a promising situation, he was soon disappointed. The news throughout the first half of 1778 was relentlessly bad for the British. France and Britain were now at war around the world, and reports had arrived that a French ship carrying thousands of veteran soldiers was making its way toward New England. An American army west of the Mississippi had crushed Britain's Native American allies. Howe's occupying force in Philadelphia had been ordered to withdraw to New York, only to be struck hard in New Jersey by a newly confident Washington, who had rolled out of Valley Forge in June. The loss of Burgoyne's army had reduced British troop strength by almost half, and the momentum in the war seemed to have shifted to the Americans and their new French allies.

Clinton's troubles were multiplied by a Parliament that had grown weary of war. More members than ever wanted to bring the fighting to a close, even if it meant negotiating with rebels. Arriving in New York in October, a British commission tried to get Congress to enter into peace talks. Emboldened by the British failures and defeats, the Americans were in no mood to talk, and the commission departed without making any progress. Parliament also let Clinton know that further spending on the war effort would be limited, and new troop assignments would not be made. Clinton, in essence, was on his own to do the best he could with the resources at his disposal. Now, as it was with Washington in 1776, the war was Clinton's to win or lose. He aimed to win it.

Doing this meant moving south. Clinton and his new subordinate, Cornwallis, felt certain that a British army operating in the southern colonies would be able to supply itself with troops and weapons drawn directly from American soil. Both generals believed that the majority of people in the South were loyal to the crown and would readily offer support and fighting forces to any British commander. As Germain stated, "Large numbers of the inhabitants [of the South] would flock to the King's standard and … His Majesty's Government would be restored."[75] It was true that an attempt to take Charleston, South Carolina (then called Charles Town), in 1776 had failed miserably, but Clinton attributed that to lack of will and competence on Howe's part. Clinton was sure that he would succeed where his predecessor had not. A powerful force under Cornwallis's command would land in the Carolinas. From there, the Regulars would move inland, where it was believed they would be welcomed as liberators by the loyal people yearning to escape from "Congress's tyranny."[76] Along the way, Cornwallis's army would destroy the rebels and establish a solid base of operations for the conquest of the northern colonies, including New England.

The Southern Campaign Starts

In November 1778, Clinton sent an invasion force south from New York with orders to capture the city of Savannah, Georgia. The soldiers would be assisted by British troops marching north from Florida. The advance north was more rapid than even Clinton expected. The units from New York linked up easily with their fellow British troops. Savannah was quickly cleared of rebels, and the British general in charge could report triumphantly on December 29 that "the capital of Georgia ... fell into our possession before it was dark."[77] One of his American opponents, commenting on the minimal British casualties, noted that "never was a victory of such magnitude so completely gained with so little loss."[78] Augusta, Georgia, fell to the British a month later. By early February 1779, Georgia was under British control, and Clinton began to plan what he hoped would be his masterstroke, which was an invasion of the Carolinas.

The next spring and summer were given over to preparations for the shift of British forces southward. Clinton planned to hold New York City with a force sufficient to keep Washington occupied, while sending warships and thousands of men to attack and "possibly get possession of Charlestown."[79] If his scheme worked, the war might end as early as the middle of 1780. As he departed New York City on December 29, 1779, Clinton had no idea that a new kind of war was about to begin.

Chapter Six

WAR IN THE SOUTH

As the American Revolution continued and the focus shifted toward the South, the way the war was fought began to change. Large battles and major sieges still took place, and the British emerged victorious in more than one of these events. However, much of the fighting in the South was done on a smaller scale; American soldiers used the element of surprise to attack British forces in a style that would come to be known as guerrilla warfare.

Clinton and his fellow British leaders did not anticipate the toll this type of fighting would take on their troops. They were not prepared to fight an entirely new kind of war on what was essentially foreign soil. They were aided by loyalists who knew the country well, but that was not enough to win the kind of decisive victory Clinton needed.

The king, Parliament, and the British public had grown tired of the war. As such, Clinton felt immense pressure to use the southern campaign to finally put an end to the American Revolution. Ultimately, that was exactly what happened, but it did not end with victory for the British. Instead, the southern part of the war led to Britain's defeat and the rise of the United States as a fully independent nation.

The Siege of Charleston

Clinton had chosen Charleston, South Carolina, as the point of entry for his invasion force. This was not the first time a British task force had targeted Charleston. In 1776, an assault was turned back in the face of fierce American resistance. Clinton had studied that earlier effort and decided to alter one crucial detail in the repeat performance. Rather than attacking from the sea, the general planned to land his troops outside the city and march into Charleston. He accomplished this

Shown here is a map of Charleston and the surrounding areas. The map was made in 1780, which was the year the city fell to the British.

soon after coming ashore in early 1780. Starting in earnest in April of that year, Clinton essentially cut the major port city off. Once in position, British engineers began constructing a series of trenches that would protect the rest of the force as it pushed to within artillery range of Charleston. Meanwhile, the British fleet closed off the shipping routes into the city. Clinton now intended to pound Charleston into submission.

Inside the beleaguered port city, the American commander General Benjamin Lincoln was confident that he could hold out. His defenses were well prepared, and he had an escape route. A small mounted force of Continentals held an important road open 30 miles (48 km) north of the city for Lincoln and the Charleston defenders if they needed it to escape. As long as the cavalry was in place, Lincoln could sit and wait.

Clinton had other ideas. After learning of the existence of the covering force, he dispatched Lieutenant Colonel Banastre Tarleton and his Green Dragoons, otherwise known as the British Legion, to destroy it. Tarleton was a daring officer known for his ferocity, intelligence, and fighting skills. His unit consisted of British cavalry and loyalist horsemen who despised the rebellion and wanted nothing more than to kill men they considered to be criminals and traitors. On April 13, Tarleton swooped down on the Americans and crushed them in what is known as the Battle of Monck's Corner. Tarleton recorded how American "officers and men who attempted to defend themselves were killed,"[80] often with bayonets. Others fled to the surrounding swamps, where they were hunted down. The luckiest of the Americans hid in the woods until nightfall and then slipped away.

When news of the defeat reached Lincoln, he immediately knew that he could no longer resist Clinton's siege. The

British cannons were firing on Charleston, and every route out of the city had been severed by British troops or ships. The American general William Moultrie described the bombardment that took place on May 7:

> *The fire was incessant almost the whole night, cannon balls whizzing and shells hissing continually among us, ammunition chests and temporary magazines blowing up, great guns exploding, and wounded men groaning along the lines. It was a dreadful night! It was our last great effort, but it availed us nothing.*[81]

Five days later, Lincoln and his troops surrendered to Clinton. Charleston had fallen, and the Carolinas lay open to the British.

A Crisis in Camden

Clinton was now free to move inland and begin the campaign he had longed to set in motion. However, he was prevented from leading the upcoming fight himself. The general's intelligence officers reported that a French fleet was headed toward New York, forcing him to return to his base in the North. Clinton put 4,000 men aboard ships and sailed away from Charleston, leaving Cornwallis and Tarleton to conduct operations as they saw fit. It was then that the war turned in a bloody new direction. The British commanders went their own ways. Cornwallis began preparing to move on the American main force near Camden, South Carolina; Tarleton made it his mission to hunt down rebel militias and slaughter them.

While Cornwallis organized his army, Tarleton and his Green Dragoons rode to Waxhaw Creek, which was near the border with North Carolina. There he overwhelmed American soldiers, who promptly surrendered. Yet, instead of collecting the men together as prisoners of war, Tarleton ordered his horsemen to cut the Americans down. The dragoons showed no mercy. The defenseless men were attacked with British bayonets. The British then went over the bodies, "plunging their bayonets into everyone that exhibited any signs of life."[82] The massacre at Waxhaw Creek earned Tarleton the nickname "Bloody Ban," and it would not be the last time that men trying to surrender would suffer such a fate. Tarleton's brutality unleashed forces of disorder and mayhem that would prove difficult for both sides to restrain.

While Tarleton was busy earning his nickname, Cornwallis marched against the American forces at Camden. His opponents comprised something less than an army. When Gates—the hero of Saratoga—took command of the Continentals who would oppose the British in South Carolina, they numbered only 1,400 weary men. Throughout the summer of 1780, Gates worked to get his troops into fighting condition. In early August, Gates's ranks grew with the arrival of about 2,000 North Carolina militiamen and a contingent of militiamen from Virginia. By the middle of the month, the

American commander felt confident that he could take on and defeat Cornwallis's advancing redcoats.

Gates's men were determined to fight, but their general had planned the upcoming battle poorly. When Gates met Cornwallis, he placed his militia rather than his better-trained Continentals opposite hardened Regulars. In the fight that followed, the British smashed through the militia and threatened to encircle the entire American army. At the mere sight of Cornwallis's men, the militiamen from North Carolina and Virginia panicked and ran. The Continentals held on a little longer, but soon they, too, were in full retreat. No American on the field that day fled as quickly as Gates himself. He mounted the fastest horse he could find and rode away from his command. By nightfall, Gates had covered 60 miles (96.6 km) in headlong flight. General Washington's young aide, Alexander Hamilton, asked bitterly, "Was there ever an instance of a general running away … from his whole army?"[83] Gates's performance at Camden was an embarrassment, and his defeat opened the way for Cornwallis to advance through the Carolinas and perhaps into Virginia. Desperate times had returned for the rebellion.

Benedict Arnold

The sting of Camden was aggravated by events far to the north in New York. Benedict Arnold had always been a proud man, but his success at Saratoga left him with an inflated sense of achievement. Arnold felt that he deserved a much

The name "Benedict Arnold" has come to mean "traitor" in the United States, but before he began dealing with the British, he was considered a war hero.

greater share of the prestige and power that went to men such as Washington. He began to imagine that Congress held a grudge against him and blamed that for his failure to rise in rank. Arnold also considered his assignments after Saratoga to be calculated insults, none more so than his appointment as commander of the fort at West Point. Arnold viewed the assignment as beneath him, and his wife encouraged his sense of injury.

Peggy Shippen Arnold was a beautiful girl whom Arnold had met in Philadelphia after the British evacuated the city. She had always harbored secret loyalist sympathies and now began to prod her husband to avenge his honor. Mrs. Arnold had already introduced her husband to a British officer named Major John André, who made it clear to the American general that aiding the crown would be the best way to get back at Washington and Congress. The command position at West Point provided Arnold with an opportunity to take André up on his offer.

By mid-September 1780, Arnold had given André the plans to the fort and had agreed to open its defenses to a British attack that very month. A British seizure of West Point would have erased any hope Washington had of eventually recapturing New York City. This fact made Arnold's treason all the more dangerous.

The plot was foiled on September 25. After a secret meeting with André, Arnold prepared for an inspection of West Point by none other than George Washington. When the commander in chief arrived, however, Arnold was nowhere to be found. His soldiers reported that he had left in a hurry before Washington got there, taking only a few personal items and saying a quick goodbye to his wife and child. The general inspected West Point as planned and was disturbed to find it in disrepair and its defenses weak. This puzzled Washington. Arnold had always been such a precise man; Washington could not figure out why the fort was in such a sorry state.

His answer came in a set of papers brought to him by his aide, Hamilton. André had been captured by an American patrol after leaving West Point. The plans to the fort and details of Arnold's treachery were discovered inside one of his boots. Arnold, having heard of the arrest before Washington showed up, was safely aboard a British warship when his commander learned of his plot to betray America. "My God!" Washington exclaimed, "Arnold has gone over to the British. Whom can we trust now?"[84]

His scheme uncovered, Arnold had no choice but to do the best he could as a newly loyal British subject. He took a command position with the British forces and prepared to serve in Virginia wearing a red coat. His wife and son were heartbroken by his departure but were treated well by the Americans, on Washington's orders. André was not so lucky. He had been captured in civilian clothes, which, by the laws of war, made him a spy. He was hanged after putting the rope around his own neck and telling his executioners, "Only bear witness that I died a brave man."[85]

American Victories

As André was being executed, the southern war began in earnest. Tarleton had always operated semi-independently from Cornwallis. Both officers agreed that while Cornwallis tackled the Continental forces, Tarleton would throw his dragoons into the struggle against the rebel militias. The ruthlessness of Tarleton and his loyalist troops was seen as

A Spy on the Inside

Spies and informants on both sides played an important role throughout the American Revolution. One of the most interesting stories of American espionage, or spying, involves Hercules Mulligan. He was a tailor who made and sold clothes in a store frequented by British officers. Mulligan was a true rebel who had been a part of the Sons of Liberty and eventually used his business relationship with the British to help the American cause. While measuring British officers for uniforms, Mulligan gathered information from them. He also paid attention to the dates British soldiers needed their mended uniforms returned, because that was often the day troops would move to a new location. Mulligan would send his slave, Cato, to George Washington with the news he learned. In one instance, the information actually helped Washington avoid capture. Although some Americans thought Mulligan was too close to the British officers, men such as Washington and Hamilton knew the truth: He was a secret hero. After the war ended, Washington had Mulligan make him clothes to prove to his fellow citizens that the tailor was to be trusted.

the only antidote to the mobile irregular, or guerrilla, warfare that plagued the southern campaign. Cornwallis's supply lines and rear areas were never safe from the rebel bands that roamed the countryside. Rebel fighters conducted hit-and-run attacks wherever and whenever they could, and their efforts were paying off. Cornwallis was compelled to slow his march through the backcountry as he dealt with the irritating rebel raids. Tarleton was assigned to suppress the rebel marauders any way he could.

The first step, Tarleton decided, was to deal with the better-organized militia forces first, leaving the loosely structured guerilla units for later. He gave this job to Major Patrick Ferguson, a solid officer who commanded a force of Regulars and loyalists. Ferguson aggressively sought battle with the rebels and finally fought them in October 1780 at Kings Mountain in South Carolina. Fighting a pitched battle with rebel militiamen, Ferguson's troops were defeated. In retaliation for Tarleton's brutality, the victorious American rebels slaughtered any American loyalists taken prisoner. Kings Mountain was a brutal example of how closely the southern war resembled a civil war.

Despite its bloody finale, the battle of Kings Mountain energized the American forces in the Carolinas. Guerilla attacks against British troops increased dramatically. Irregular units commanded by men such as Francis Marion, known as the "Swamp Fox," and Thomas Sumter, often called the "Carolina Gamecock," took a steady toll on Cornwallis's expedition and eventually became ever bolder. Rebel militias attacked their loyalist counterparts relentlessly. So many Americans were killing each other that one loyalist reported that South Carolina "resembled a piece of patchwork,"[86] with neighbor fighting neighbor.

American successes in late 1780 also encouraged the aggressiveness of Gates's replacements in the Carolinas, General Nathanael Greene and his able assistant, Daniel Morgan. Greene and Morgan had been assigned the difficult task of keeping Cornwallis from extending his reach northward into North Carolina and Virginia. Given the right circumstances and a sound plan, the two Americans were certain that they could do just that. The first step would be to force Tarleton to suspend his irregular operations and rejoin Cornwallis's main army. Then, the British Regulars and Tarleton's dragoons could be defeated at once, leaving the Carolinas in the hands of the Continental army. Boldness and daring were called for, and Greene and Morgan had plenty of both.

The Road to Yorktown

Violating a typical rule of war, Greene and Morgan divided their forces during the winter of 1780 to 1781 and went looking for their enemies. Greene, it was planned, would handle Cornwallis while Morgan took care of diverting the attention of Tarleton's mobile forces. Neither Greene nor Morgan ever imagined that Tarleton's legion would be brought to battle and nearly annihilated. However, that is exactly what happened. On January 17, 1781, Morgan met Tarleton near the border between North Carolina and South Carolina.

The place was called Cowpens, and it was perfectly suited for the type of combat Morgan preferred. Backed up against the water, his less-than-reliable militia would be forced to fight hard, but that did not really matter to Morgan. He expected the militia line to break when Tarleton's British Regulars and loyalists struck it. That is why he placed his trustworthy Continentals in a camouflaged position behind the militia. Once in position, Morgan waited for the British to assemble and prepared for Tarleton's charge. When it came, Morgan broke it and sent Tarleton's men reeling backward. By noon, the battle was over. More than 100 British soldiers were killed and hundreds more were taken prisoner. With a mere 40 cavalrymen, Tarleton limped back to Cornwallis to report on his defeat.

Cornwallis was now more determined than ever to smash Greene and Morgan. He immediately set out after the Americans, who had brought their commands back together, and caught them on March 15, 1781, at Guilford Courthouse in North Carolina. However, Cornwallis caught hold of more than he could handle. He had with him about 2,000 troops, compared to

This artwork shows officers fighting during the Battle of Cowpens.

nearly 4,500 Americans. For once, Greene and Morgan had the advantage. They intended to use it. Morgan urged Greene to replay the Battle of Cowpens. "Put the riflemen on the flanks," he advised. "Put the militia in the centre, with some picked troops in their rear with orders to shoot down the first man that runs."[87] Greene

80 *The American Revolution: Fighting for Independence*

The True Story of the "Swamp Fox"

The famous 2000 movie *The Patriot* offered a fictionalized account of guerrilla warfare in the South during the American Revolution. More specifically, the film broadly traced the life of the South Carolina rebel guerrilla leader Francis Marion, who was nicknamed the "Swamp Fox." Although the Hollywood version of Francis Marion fought only for liberty, the real-life guerrilla and his men often had less heroic goals. Looting, stealing loyalist land, and settling personal scores proved many times to be more important to them than independence. Men such as Marion, in fact, rarely acted the part of noble soldiers and matched the brutality of their opponents. American guerrillas killed prisoners, burned homes, and terrorized innocent people. However, they did prove to be essential parts of the American war effort. The activities of rebel bands, such as the ones led by Marion, hindered British operations and helped to force decisive battles, such as Cowpens, Guilford Courthouse, and Yorktown.

Francis Marion (the "Swamp Fox")

War in the South 81

took this advice and arranged his defenses in three separate lines with militia in the front and Continentals in the rear.

Eager for battle, Cornwallis launched his force directly at the Americans. Through a hail of musket balls, the British rushed forward. When the first line finally broke, the redcoats pushed on toward the second, which collapsed. At the third line, however, the Americans stood their ground, trading vicious fire with their British opponents. Cornwallis himself had a horse shot out from under him but continued to lead his troops forward. Pouring artillery fire into the American line, the British fought furiously. Finally, Greene, fearing his army might collapse, ordered a general retreat.

Cornwallis won, but his men were too exhausted to pursue their foes. On April 25, Cornwallis left a small army behind to harass the Americans and took the bulk of his ravaged forces into Virginia. There he planned to rest and resupply his troops, then join up with Arnold, who had been newly commissioned a brigadier general, in a quest to conquer Virginia and clear the Carolinas of rebels. Cornwallis wanted to remain in the interior of Virginia, but Clinton had other considerations. He needed Cornwallis's army to be close to the sea, just in case New York came under attack. Clinton suggested that Cornwallis choose a base of operations closer to navigable rivers and the Chesapeake Bay. The spot that best fit that description was the peninsula between the York River and the James River, in particular the port of Yorktown, Virginia.

"The World Turned Upside Down"

By the end of July 1781, Cornwallis had finished gathering his troops at Yorktown and had completed a series of impressive fortifications around it. At the same time, Washington was conducting minor operations around New York while waiting for a French fleet to arrive that would bring thousands of French soldiers to his command. The previous May, he and the French general Jean-Baptiste-Donatien de Vimeur, comte de Rochambeau, had decided to attack Clinton as soon as the reinforcements arrived. When the two learned of Cornwallis's movement, however, they sent a message to the admiral in command, François-Joseph-Paul, comte de Grasse, to turn his ships toward the Chesapeake Bay and meet them there. The French-American army then slipped quietly away from its station around New York City and marched toward Yorktown.

Washington left men along the Hudson River to hide his movement and took about 5,000 French soldiers and about 2,000 American soldiers south with him. By early September, with his army nearing Virginia, Washington learned that part of Cornwallis's command had been shipped back to New York to reinforce Clinton. Hearing this, the general increased the pace of his march. Meanwhile, the French fleet arrived, and 3,000 French soldiers landed near Yorktown. They immediately linked up with a small contingent of Americans, led by Lafayette, who had been monitoring Cornwallis. Sensing trouble, Clinton ordered

This 19th-century lithograph shows Washginton accepting the British surrender at Yorktown.

Strength at Sea

Credit for helping America win its independence is most often given to the French army and its celebrated officers, including Rochambeau and Lafayette. A group of French naval officers, however, are perhaps more worthy of that honor. Ships under the command of men such as Charles-Hector, comte d'Estaing, and François-Joseph-Paul, comte de Grasse, played a crucial role in the war, in particular at the Battle of Yorktown. When Grasse's fleet appeared in the Chesapeake Bay, it signaled the end of Cornwallis's southern campaign. Grasse sealed off Cornwallis's only escape route and completed the encirclement of the British begun by Washington and Rochambeau. The French warships then turned back a relief force commanded by the British admiral Sir Thomas Graves, winning arguably the most important naval battle of the war. The size and obvious power of Grasse's fleet persuaded General Clinton that any further effort to rescue Cornwallis would be a waste of energy and resources. Without hope from the sea, Cornwallis was compelled to surrender. As powerful as it was, the combined French-American army could not have won at Yorktown without the French naval forces.

---

a fleet southward to rescue Cornwallis, but it arrived too late. On September 5, the French navy turned the British ships back at the Battle of the Capes. Cornwallis was on his own. Washington and Rochambeau arrived on September 28 and laid siege to Yorktown with a mighty army of more than 16,000 men.

For more than a month, the French and American artillery pounded Cornwallis's positions. Fierce counterattacks by the British failed to break through the allied lines on land, and no relief fleet could break in from the sea. The British were trapped. As the days passed, conditions inside Yorktown worsened. Food supplies ran low; the wounded suffered without medicine or proper care. Worst of all, the incoming artillery fire was unrelenting. A doctor accompanying Washington wrote that "a tremendous and incessant firing from the American and French batteries is kept up, and the enemy return the fire, but with little effect."[88] On the other side of the trenches, the British complained that they "could find no refuge in or out of the town. The people fled to the waterside and hid in hastily contrived shelters on the banks, but many of them were killed by bursting bombs."[89]

Cornwallis had no choice. His lines were crumbling, and soon the French and Americans would punch their way in. On October 17, he dispatched an officer carrying a white flag to speak with Washington about terms of surrender. As Cornwallis later told Clinton, he saw it as "wanton and inhuman ... to sacrifice the lives of [his] gallant soldiers ... by exposing them to an assault which, from the numbers and precautions of the enemy, could not fail to succeed."[90] Washington received the British officer and informed him that his commander could sign surrender papers in the morning.

The British flags were rolled up, and the army's weapons were stacked in front of the French-American lines. The British marched out of Yorktown on October 19, 1781. Cornwallis was not with them. He claimed to be too sick to attend the ceremonies and left it to one of his aides to surrender the army. His replacement, General Charles O'Hara, offered his sword to Rochambeau at first. It was refused; the French general pointed to Washington. When O'Hara approached Washington and once again held out the blade, the general said courteously, "Never from such a good hand,"[91] and motioned toward Lincoln, who accepted it. As the redcoats sadly filed forward and stacked their arms, the band played a tune everyone recognized called "The World Turned Upside Down." The words came to the minds of all present at Yorktown:

If ponies rode men and if grass ate cows,
And cats should be chased into holes by the mouse ...
If summer were spring and the other way round,
Then all the world would be upside down.

When Clinton was informed of Cornwallis's surrender, he knew the war was lost. The world truly had been turned upside down by a group of determined patriots and their French allies.

Epilogue

A NEW NATION

Many believe the American Revolution ended with the British surrender at Yorktown. However, the war continued for another two years after Cornwallis's defeat in Virginia. While Clinton was virtually trapped with the remnants of the British forces in New York City, battles were still being fought around the world. The expansion of the American Revolution into a global conflict meant the war did not automatically end when fighting in America stopped. Instead, both Clinton and Washington waited for the fighting to stop in places far from where it began.

When the American Revolution finally ended, this war that began as a conflict within one empire had affected the entire world. It ushered in a new age of democratic revolutions and the weakening of empires around the globe. It also gave birth to a nation that rose from a small band of 13 colonies struggling to claim its independence to a world power defined by its fight for freedom.

War Around the World

Before peace came to America, it had to be secured overseas and in the Caribbean. By the end of 1781, the land war in America was essentially over. However, the war at sea was just heating up. Naval battles did not play a major part in the early years of the war, but they were a massive component of its final phase.

Another key player entered the fighting during this last part of the American Revolution. Spain was an ally of France and an enemy of Britain, so it joined the war in 1779 on the side of the United States. Although Spain did not develop a close relationship with America the same way France did, its participation in the conflict was important. It further weakened the British war effort. Historian John Shy stated that when Spain entered the war,

The Great Siege of Gibraltar, shown here, diverted British attention and resources away from North America at a crucial time during the American Revolution.

it "set off a new wave of panic in London and New York."[92] British leaders believed that adding another foreign foe to the mix would take resources and energy away from the main conflict in America, which was proving to be more difficult to win than anyone had thought. These leaders were right.

Spanish aid came mainly in the form of its navy. The combined forces of the French and Spanish battled the British in the waters around South Africa, India, and the West Indies. They also struck the British at Gibraltar on the Mediterranean Sea. The Siege of Gibraltar—sometimes called The Great Siege of Gibraltar—lasted for more than three years. Although the British ultimately remained in control of their fortress there, victory came at a cost. Historian Geoffrey Perret explained, "The British held on to Gibraltar and lost America."[93] By directing troops, supplies, and attention toward this and other battles at sea, the British were unable to throw their full military might into the fighting on American soil. Britain had to divide its resources, but America could rely on its new allies for help overseas.

A New Nation **87**

America was able to slip out of Britain's grasp while Britain was busy fighting France and Spain.

Peace in Paris

War was still raging on the seas, but it became clear to British leaders that it was time to begin peace talks and seek an end to this conflict, which had left them humiliated. North's government fell apart, and William Petty-Fitzmaurice, who was also known as the earl of Shelburne, replaced him as prime minister. Shelburne worked on a peace agreement between Britain and the nations it was at war with—including the United States.

By November 1782, British and American negotiators came to an agreement. The Americans made sure that the agreement included Britain's acknowledgment of their new independence. However, the agreement was considered preliminary rather than a formal treaty because Britain and France had not yet reached a place of peace. The alliance between the United States and France allowed for separate negotiations with Britain but not a separate peace, so the Americans waited.

France and Spain were finally ready to sign peace treaties with Britain on September 3, 1783. That day, three treaties were signed. The treaty between the United States and Britain is known as the Treaty of Paris, because that is where it was signed. The following year, Britain signed a peace treaty with the Netherlands, which had also entered this international conflict.

The Treaty of Paris called for both sides to pay off debts owed to creditors before the war. It also called for the protection of loyalists in the United States. In addition, Britain was able to keep control of Canada. Although France had hoped to win back its Canadian lands through this war, it still agreed to these peace terms.

In return, Britain promised to remove its troops from America, beginning with those stationed in New York City. It also gave the United States western lands, which extended its borders to the Atlantic Ocean in the East and the Mississippi River in the West. Finally, Britain formally recognized American independence. The patriots had achieved what they began fighting for almost a decade earlier. The United States of America was finally recognized as its own free and independent nation, and Americans were no longer under British control. The American Revolution was over, and a future full of new possibilities lay ahead for this new nation.

Challenges and Changes

The United States was now its own nation, and with independence came a new set of challenges. Following the American Revolution, anti-American leaders in Britain created trade policies designed to limit American commerce. The British also refused to abandon a number of forts on American soil, which was a direct violation of the Treaty of Paris. In addition to problems with the British, the Americans also struggled in their early dealings with Spain. Because Spain was no longer connected to the United States by war, it did not hesitate to create policies designed to

without Difficulty and without requiring any Compensation.

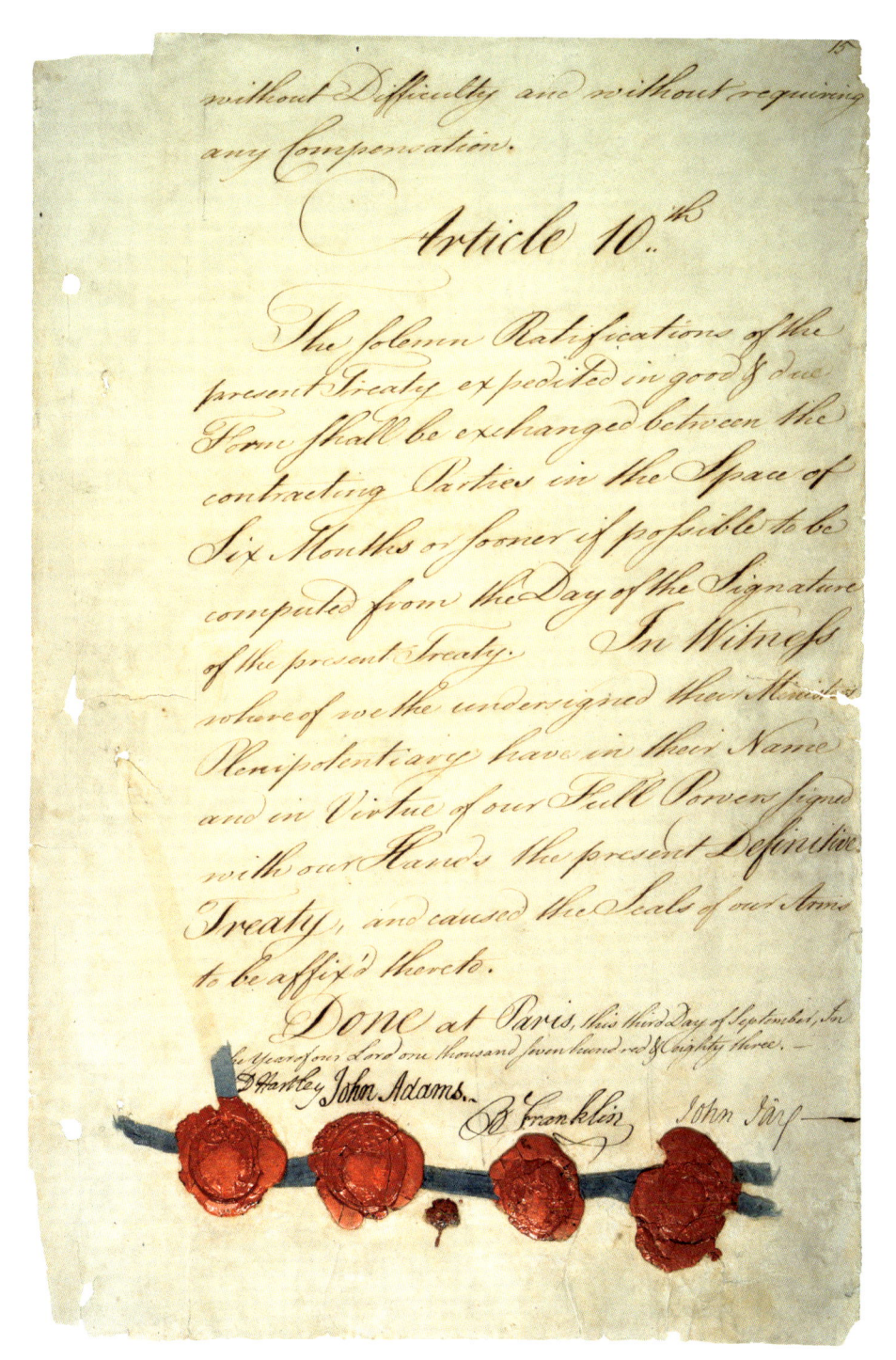

Article 10th

The solemn Ratifications of the present Treaty expedited in good & due Form shall be exchanged between the contracting Parties in the Space of Six Months or sooner if possible to be computed from the Day of the Signature of the present Treaty. In Witness whereof we the undersigned their Ministers Plenipotentiary have in their Name and in Virtue of our Full Powers signed with our Hands the present Definitive Treaty, and caused the Seals of our Arms to be affix'd thereto. Done at Paris, this third Day of September, In the Year of our Lord one thousand seven hundred & eighty three.

D Hartley   John Adams.   B Franklin   John Jay

Shown here is the last page of the Treaty of Paris, which officially ended the American Revolution.

benefit its economy at the expense of the United States. For example, the Spanish controlled all traffic along the Mississippi River and closed it off to American trading vessels.

The American economy was already struggling, and it owed many debts to foreign countries that offered aid during the American Revolution. Instead of a strong central response to this crisis, Americans were left with a federal government that had little power to affect change. Under the Articles of Confederation, the U.S. government could not raise national taxes or armies. It had to depend on the states to do those things, and it could not enforce its policies or make the states cooperate. This government inspired very little faith in the American people. They felt their central government could not protect them from outside threats or economic collapse.

Why, then, did U.S. leaders create such a weak central government? The Articles of Confederation were a response to the problems that led to the American Revolution. Americans were so afraid to give a central government too much power that they veered too far in the other direction. In trying to avoid the kind of tyranny they broke away from during the war, they were left with a central government that was essentially powerless.

Americans realized things needed to change after an uprising led by Massachusetts veteran Daniel Shays. The federal government had no way to respond to such an uprising, and that concerned many Americans, including George Washington. In a letter to his wartime artillery chief, Henry Knox, Washington wrote, "I feel, my dear General Knox, infinitely more than I can express to you, for the disorders which have arisen in these States. Good God!"[94] Washington believed that signs of weakness such as Shays's Rebellion made America look weak to Britain, which was still working to cause problems in the new nation: " … She is at this moment sowing the seeds of jealousy and discontent among the various tribes of Indians on our frontiers."[95] Washington believed America could not afford to look vulnerable at such an early stage in its history, and he was certainly not the only one who advocated for change.

The U.S. Constitution

In May 1787, a convention began to revise the Articles of Confederation. As the meetings went on, however, it became clear that an entirely new document—and a new governing structure—was needed. During what became known as the Constitutional Convention, the delegates debated and compromised until they drafted a new U.S. Constitution. This document gave the federal government more power than it had under the Articles, especially in the areas of foreign and economic policy. The U.S. Constitution quelled Americans' fears of tyranny by creating three branches of government that worked through a system of checks and balances. The judicial branch was led by the U.S. Supreme Court, and the legislative branch was made up of a Congress

The U.S. Constitution, shown here, was amended soon after it was adopted to include a Bill of Rights, which protected individual liberties and guarded against tyranny.

divided into two parts: the Senate and the House of Representatives.

The final branch of the U.S. federal government was the executive branch. Its leader would be called the president, and it was clear to many in America who the nation's first president should be. In 1789, George Washington was elected to serve as the first president of the United States. Washington's reputation as the heroic leader of the American Revolution made him popular with the masses. Americans trusted Washington, and they respected him. They saw him as a leader who fought for their liberty and would protect it as America carved out its own identity.

The Fight for Freedom Continues

The American Revolution sent shockwaves around the world. The American patriots became examples for many people who wanted to fight back against what they saw as oppressive governments. Even America's ally in their fight for freedom, France, was swept up in revolutionary fever less than a decade after the end of the American Revolution.

However, this war did not grant freedom to all Americans. It took almost another century—after the conclusion of the American Civil War—before the practice of slavery in the United States finally ended. Even after that, the fight for freedom continued. The spirit of the American Revolution was felt—and still can be felt—in every battle for freedom and equality fought in the United States. The women's suffrage movement of the early 20th century, the civil rights movement of the 1960s, and the fight for equal rights for members of the LGBT community all have their roots in the belief that Americans have always fought for liberty when it is threatened. This belief is older than the nation itself. It started with a group of British colonists who wanted the chance to control their own government, and more than 200 years later, that belief is still alive and well in the nation they fought to create.

Notes

Introduction: A Growing Divide

1. Jack P. Greene, ed., *Settlements to Society, 1607–1763: A Documentary History of Colonial America*. New York, NY: W.W. Norton, 1975, p. 8.
2. John J. McCusker, and Russell R. Menard, *The Economy of British America, 1607–1789*. Chapel Hill, NC: University of North Carolina Press, 1985, p. 39.
3. Edmund Morgan, *Inventing the People: The Rise of Popular Sovereignty in England and America*. New York, NY: W.W. Norton, 1988, p. 133.
4. Quoted in John Ferling, *Struggle for a Continent: The Wars of Early America*. Arlington Heights, IL: Harlan Davidson, 1993, p. 205.
5. Quoted in Ferling, *Struggle for a Continent*, p. 206.

Chapter One: Tightening Control

6. Henry Steele Commager, ed., *Documents of American History*. New York, NY: Appleton-Century-Crofts, 1958, p. 47.
7. Quoted in Commager, *Documents of American History*, p. 49.
8. Quoted in Commager, *Documents of American History*, p. 50.
9. Quoted in A.J. Langguth, *Patriots: The Men Who Started the American Revolution*. New York, NY: Simon & Schuster, 1988, p. 49.
10. Quoted in Commager, *Documents of American History*, p. 56.
11. Quoted in Commager, *Documents of American History*, p. 58.
12. Bernard Bailyn, The *Ordeal of Thomas Hutchinson*. Cambridge, MA: Belknap Press of the Harvard University Press, 1974, p. 37.
13. Quoted in Bailyn, *Ordeal of Thomas Hutchinson*, p. 36.
14. Quoted in Bailyn, *Ordeal of Thomas Hutchinson*, p. 110.
15. Quoted in Commager, *Documents of American History*, p. 61.

Chapter Two: Taxes and Bloodshed

16. Quoted in Commager, *Documents of American History*, p. 63.
17. Quoted in Robert Harvey, *"A Few Bloody Noses": The Realities and Myths of the American Revolution*. New York, NY: Overlook, 2001, p. 79.
18. Quoted in Commager, *Documents of American History*, p. 66.
19. Quoted in Robert Middlekauff, *The Glorious Cause: The American Revolution, 1763–1789*. New York,

NY: Oxford University Press, 1982, p. 169.
20. Quoted in Langguth, *Patriots*, p. 101.
21. Quoted in Bailyn, *Ordeal of Thomas Hutchinson*, p. 123.
22. Quoted in Benson Bobrick, *Angel in the Whirlwind: The Triumph of the American Revolution*. New York, NY: Simon & Schuster, 1997, pp. 82–83.
23. Quoted in Bobrick, *Angel in the Whirlwind*, p. 83.
24. Quoted in Harvey, "A Few Bloody Noses," p. 101.
25. Quoted in Langguth, *Patriots*, p. 131.
26. Quoted in Middlekauff, *Glorious Cause*, p. 182.
27. Quoted in Langguth, *Patriots*, p. 105.
28. Quoted in Langguth, *Patriots*, p. 137.
29. Quoted in Langguth, *Patriots*, p. 137.
30. Jack P. Greene, ed., *Colonies to Nation, 1763–1789: A Documentary History of the American Revolution*. New York, NY: W.W. Norton, 1975, p. 196.

Chapter Three: From Boston Harbor to Lexington and Concord

31. Quoted in Harvey, "A Few Bloody Noses," p. 112.
32. Quoted in Langguth, *Patriots*, p. 176.
33. Quoted in Langguth, *Patriots*, p. 177.
34. Quoted in Langguth, *Patriots*, p. 181.
35. Quoted in Langguth, *Patriots*, p. 181.
36. Quoted in Commager, *Documents of American History*, p. 71.
37. Quoted in Bobrick, *Angel in the Whirlwind*, p. 92.
38. Quoted in Bobrick, *Angel in the Whirlwind*, p. 95.
39. Quoted in Bobrick, *Angel in the Whirlwind*, p. 93.
40. Quoted in Greene, *Colonies to Nation*, p. 249.
41. Quoted in Middlekauff, *Glorious Cause*, p. 262.
42. Quoted in Harvey, "A Few Bloody Noses," p. 99.
43. George F. Scheer and Hugh F. Rankin, eds., *Rebels and Redcoats: The American Revolution Through the Eyes of Those Who Fought and Lived It*. New York, NY: De Capo, 1957, p. 20.
44. Quoted in Scheer and Rankin, *Rebels and Redcoats*, p. 21.
45. Quoted in Langguth, *Patriots*, p. 240.
46. Quoted in Scheer and Rankin, *Rebels and Redcoats*, p. 34.
47. Quoted in Esmond Wright, ed., *The Fire of Liberty: The American War of Independence Seen Through the Eyes of the Men and Women, the Statesmen and Soldiers Who Fought It*. New York, NY: St. Martin's, 1983, p. 25.
48. Quoted in Wright, *Fire of Liberty*, p. 26.
49. Quoted in Wright, *Fire of Liberty*, p. 28.

Chapter Four: A War for Independence

50. Steven Rosswurm, *Arms, Country, and Class: The Philadelphia Militia and the "Lower Sort" During the American Revolution*. New Bruns-

wick, NJ: Rutgers University Press, 1987, p. 49.
51. Quoted in Middlekauff, *Glorious Cause*, p. 28.
52. Quoted in Scheer and Rankin, *Rebels and Redcoats*, p. 62.
53. Quoted in Scheer and Rankin, *Rebels and Redcoats*, p. 62.
54. Quoted in Scheer and Rankin, *Rebels and Redcoats*, p. 128.
55. Quoted in Greene, *Colonies to Nation*, p. 259.
56. Harvey, "*A Few Bloody Noses,*" p. 199.
57. Quoted in Greene, *Colonies to Nation*, p. 270.
58. Quoted in Greene, *Colonies to Nation*, p. 277.
59. Quoted in Greene, *Colonies to Nation*, p. 278.
60. Quoted in Greene, *Colonies to Nation*, p. 284.
61. Quoted in Greene, *Colonies to Nation*, p. 297.
62. Quoted in Scheer and Rankin, *Rebels and Redcoats*, p. 166.
63. Quoted in Wright, *Fire of Liberty*, p. 72.
64. Quoted in Greene, *Colonies to Nation*, p. 406.
65. Quoted in Langguth, *Patriots*, p. 393.

Chapter Five: A Turning Point

66. Quoted in Middlekauff, *Glorious Cause*, p. 372.
67. Quoted in Middlekauff, *Glorious Cause*, p. 385.
68. Quoted in Wright, *Fire of Liberty*, p. 94.
69. Quoted in Scheer and Rankin, *Rebels and Redcoats*, p. 275.
70. Quoted in Scheer and Rankin, *Rebels and Redcoats*, p. 276.
71. Quoted in Langguth, *Patriots*, p. 456.
72. Quoted in Langguth, *Patriots*, p. 451.
73. Quoted in Commager, *Documents of American History*, p. 106.
74. Quoted in Commager, *Documents of American History*, p. 107.
75. Quoted in Scheer and Rankin, *Rebels and Redcoats*, p. 390.
76. Quoted in Middlekauff, *Glorious Cause*, p. 437.
77. Quoted in Bobrick, *Angel in the Whirlwind*, p. 373.
78. Quoted in Bobrick, *Angel in the Whirlwind*, p. 373.
79. Quoted in Harvey, "*A Few Bloody Noses,*" p. 329.

Chapter Six: War in the South

80. Quoted in Wright, *Fire of Liberty*, p. 183.
81. Quoted in Harvey, "*A Few Bloody Noses,*" pp. 331–32.
82. Quoted in Harvey, "*A Few Bloody Noses,*" p. 333.
83. Quoted in Scheer and Rankin, *Rebels and Redcoats*, p. 410.
84. Quoted in Langguth, *Patriots*, p. 504.
85. Quoted in Langguth, *Patriots*, p. 509.
86. Quoted in Harvey, "*A Few Bloody Noses,*" p. 369.
87. Bobrick, *Angel in the Whirlwind*, p. 433.
88. Quoted in Wright, *Fire of Liberty*, p. 232.

89. Quoted in Wright, *Fire of Liberty*, p. 233.
90. Quoted in Harvey, "A Few Bloody Noses," p. 405.
91. Quoted in Langguth, *Patriots*, p. 540.

Epilogue: A New Nation

92. John Shy, *A People Numerous and Armed: Reflections on the Military Struggle for American Independence*. Ann Arbor, MI: University of Michigan Press, 1990, p. 205.
93. Geoffrey Perret, *A Country Made by War: From the Revolution to Vietnam—The Story of America's Rise to Power*. New York, NY: Random House, 1989, p. 69.
94. Quoted in Greene, *Colonies to Nation*, p. 507.
95. Quoted in Greene, *Colonies to Nation*, p. 508.

For More Information

Books

Casey, Susan. *Women Heroes of the American Revolution: 20 Stories of Espionage, Sabotage, Defiance, and Rescue*. Chicago, IL: Chicago Review Press, 2015.
Casey details the amazing accomplishments of 20 real women and girls who served their country in whatever way they could during the American Revolution, including female spies, battlefield nurses, and even secret soldiers.

Hamilton, Alexander, John Jay, and James Madison. *The Federalist Papers*. London, UK: Arcturus Publishing Limited, 2016.
The Federalist Papers is a collection of essays written by three of the most prominent Founding Fathers to defend the U.S. Constitution, and it continues to provide unique insight into this revolutionary document.

McCullough, David. *1776: The Illustrated Edition*. New York, NY: Simon & Schuster, 2005.
McCullough's comprehensive account of the year America was born is enhanced with paintings, maps, and letters, providing readers with a clear picture of the events of that year on both sides of the Atlantic Ocean.

Paine, Thomas. *Common Sense*. New York, NY: Penguin Books, 2012.
This edition of the pamphlet that was written to explain why independence was the best course of action for the colonies has a new introduction written by noted historian Richard Beeman.

Sheinkin, Steve. *The Notorious Benedict Arnold: A True Story of Adventure, Heroism, and Tragedy*. New York, NY: Roaring Book Press, 2010.
Sheinkin's biography of Benedict Arnold sheds a new and exciting light on the story of perhaps the most infamous traitor in American history.

Websites

American Revolution (www.history.com/topics/american-revolution)
The History Channel's American Revolution page features articles about the war's most notable people, places, and events, as well as a selection of relevant videos.

The American Revolution: Lighting Freedom's Flame (www.nps.gov/revwar/index.html)
The National Parks Service provides an in-depth look at the people, places, and events that shaped the American Revolution, including a list of sites you can visit to experience the locations where history was made.

The American Revolution and the New Nation, 1775–1815 (www.loc.gov/rr/program/bib/ourdocs/NewNation.html)
This list of documents compiled by the Library of Congress stands as a definitive collection of primary sources from the American Revolution and the early years of the United States.

The Charters of Freedom: "A New World Is at Hand" (www.archives.gov/exhibits/charters/)
The National Archives presents a detailed analysis of three documents that defined America during and after the American Revolution: the Declaration of Independence, the U.S. Constitution, and the Bill of Rights.

George Washington's Mount Vernon (www.mountvernon.org/)
The official website of George Washington's historic home provides the information needed to help you plan a trip to this landmark. It also provides information about Washington and his role in the American Revolution.

Index

A
Adams, John
  Boston Massacre and, 34
  First Continental Congress, 39
  Howe and, 62
  on independence, 56
Adams, Samuel
  attempted arrest of, 41–44
  radical movement and, 17–18, 26, 35
  Sugar Act and, 17–18
  Tea Act and, 18, 36–37
American Board of Customs Commissioners, 24
American Crisis, The (Paine), 59
André, John, 77
Arnold, Benedict
  Canadian campaign, 51–52
  Saratoga, 65–69
  treason by, 76–77
Arnold, Peggy Shippen, 77
Articles of Confederation, 56, 90
Attucks, Crispus, 32

B
Bailyn, Bernard, 21–22
Beaumarchais, Pierre-Augustin Caron de, 53
Beaver (ship), 36
Bemis Heights, Battle of, 67–68
Bernard, Francis
  call for British troops, 27
  dissolved Massachusetts House of Representatives, 26
  Stamp Act and, 21
Bloody Ban, 75
Bonhomme Richard (ship), 70
Boston Gazette (newspaper), 26
Boston Massacre, 30–34
Boston Port Act (1774), 38
Boston Tea Party, 18, 36–38
Breed's Hill, 49–51, 61
Britain. *See* Great Britain.
British army
  blacks in, 29
  German mercenaries, 53–54, 57
  Green Dragoons, 74–75, 77, 79
  housing in colonies of, 19, 23, 38
  Native American allies, 11, 63, 71
  opinion of colonial soldiers, 12
British Legion, 74
Brooklyn, New York, 57–58
Brown Bess, 47
Bunker Hill, Battle of, 50–51
Burgoyne, Sir John
  appointed, 61
  Breed's Hill and, 48–51
  characteristics of, 62
  strategy of, 62–63, 65–68

C
Camden, South Carolina, 75–76
Canada, 13, 51–52, 61–62, 88
Caribbean, 16, 69, 86
Carleton, Sir Guy, 61
Carolina Gamecock, the, 79
Charleston, South Carolina, 36, 71–75
Chesapeake Bay, 63, 82, 84
Clinton, Sir Henry
  appointed, 48
  Battle of Bunker Hill and, 51–52
  in command, 61
  siege of Charleston and, 73–74
  strategy of, 71–72
  Yorktown and, 82, 84–86
colonists
  divine mission of, 58
  loyalties of, 39
  Native Americans allied with, 63
  Navigation Acts and, 10
  reaction to Proclamation of 1763, 15
  reaction to Revenue Act, 26, 30
  reaction to Stamp Act, 19–21
  reaction to Sugar Act, 17–18
  reaction to Tea Act, 35–38
  sentiments about British, 8
  settlement restrictions, 13
  smuggling by, 10
  working class, 67
  see also militiamen
Common Sense (Paine), 54, 56
Concord, Massachusetts, 42–46
Constitution, 90–92
Continental army
  blacks in, 32
  training of, 68–69
  Washington chosen commander, 49
  working-class troops, 67
  see also specific battles
Continental Congress
  First, 18, 39–41
  Second, 48–53, 56–57, 63, 71
Controversy Between Great

Britain and Her Colonies Reviewed, The (Knox), 25
Convention Army, 68
Conway, Thomas, 65
Conway Cabal, 65
Cornwallis, Charles Lord
    Battle of Guilford Courthouse, 79–80
    guerrillas and, 77–78
    in South, 71–72, 75–79
    at Yorktown, 82, 84–85
Cowpens, Battle of, 79–81
Currency Act (1764), 17

D
Dartmouth, Lord, 41
Dartmouth (ship), 36–37
Dawes, William, 43
Deane, Silas, 53
Declaration of Independence (1776), 55–56, 58
Declaratory Act (1766), 23–24
Dickinson, John, 26
Dunmore, Lord, 32, 38

E
East India Company, 34–36
economy, 10, 15, 17, 21, 90
    see also trade
Eleanor (ship), 36
England. See Great Britain
Estaing, Charles-Hector Comte d', 84

F
Ferguson, Patrick, 78
First Continental Congress, 18, 39–41
Fitzmaurice, William Petty, 88
Florida, 13, 72
France
    aid from, 53, 65, 69
    defensive alliance with, 69
    Native Americans and, 11
    naval warfare, 84
    Seven Years' War, 13, 53
    troops and navy of, 69, 84
Franklin, Benjamin
    Declaration of Independence and, 56
    defensive alliance and, 69
    French aid and, 53, 65
    negotiations with Howe, 59
    taxation and, 23
French and Indian War, 11, 13, 41

G
Gage, Thomas
    arrests of Samuel Adams and John Hancock, 41–42
    Battle of Bunker Hill and, 50–51
    British loss of confidence in, 51
    on British troops, 27, 46
    relieved of command, 51, 61
    as royal governor of Massachusetts, 38
    show of troops in Boston, 41–43
Gates, Horatio, 65, 68–69, 75–76, 79
Gaustad, Edwin S., 58
George III
    Declaratory Act and, 23
    orders to suppress rebellion, 52–53
    rebellion recognized by, 41
    rejection of Olive Branch Petition, 51–53
Georgia, 30, 39, 56, 72
Germain, Lord George, 71
German mercenaries, 53–54, 57
Gibraltar, 87
Grasse, François-Joseph-Paul Comte de, 82, 84
Graves, Sir Thomas, 84
Gravier, Charles, Comte de Vergennes, 53
Great Britain
    cost of smuggling to, 10
    economy of, 9–10
    sentiments about colonists, 8
    Seven Years' War, 13, 53
    see also British Army
Green Dragoons, 74–75, 77, 79
Greene, Nathanael, 79–80, 82
Grenville, Sir George, 19, 23
guerrillas, 73, 78, 81
Guilford Courthouse, Battle of, 79–80

H
Hamilton, Alexander, 76–78
Hancock, John
    attempted arrest of, 41–42
    smuggling and, 27
Harvey, Robert, 53
Hessians, 54, 60
House of Burgesses (Virginia), 19–20
Howe, Richard, 59
Howe, Sir William
    appointed, 48
    attack on Philadelphia, 62–63, 65
    Battle of Bunker Hill and, 50–51
    characteristics of, 61–62
    evacuated Boston, 53
    negotiations with Americans, 59
    in New York City, 57–60
    relieved of command, 71
Hutchinson, Thomas
    Boston Massacre and, 33–34
    as governor, 22, 35
    loyalist, 22
    Stamp Act and, 21

I
immigrants, 39
India, 69, 87
Intolerable Acts (1774), 38, 40–41
Iroquois (Haudenosaunee), 62

J
Jefferson, Thomas, 55–56, 58
Jones, John Paul, 70

K
Kings Mountain, Battle of, 78–79
Knox, William, 25

L
Lafayette, Marquis de, 68–69, 82, 84
Lee, Arthur, 53
Lee, Charles, 57, 59
Lee, Richard Henry, 56
legislative sovereignty, 10
Letters from a Pennsylvania Farmer (Dickinson), 26
Lexington, Massachusetts, 42–44
Liberty (ship), 27
Lincoln, Benjamin, 74–75, 85
Livingston, Robert, 56
lobsterbacks, 29, 46
  see also British Army
Long Island, Battle of, 58–59
Louis XVI (king of France), 53, 69
loyalists
  German mercenaries and, 54
  new immigrants as, 39
  in South, 73–74, 77–79
  see also Hutchinson, Thomas
Loyal Nine, 18

M
Marion, Francis, 79, 81
Maryland, 49
Massachusetts
  Lexington and Concord, 42–46
  measures against, 21, 38–39
  reaction to Revenue Act, 26, 30
  reaction to Stamp Act, 20–21, 23
  reaction to Tea Act, 36–38
Massachusetts Government Act (1774), 38
Massachusetts Provincial Congress, 41, 45
McCusker, John J., 10, 16
Menard, Russell R., 10, 16
militiamen, 12, 41, 44–45, 48, 67, 75–76, 78
"midnight ride," 42, 43
Minutemen, 44–46
Mississippi River, 13, 71, 88, 90
molasses, 10, 15–18, 23
Molasses Act (1733), 15–16
Montgomery, Richard, 51
Montreal, Canada, 51
Morgan, Daniel, 65, 79–80
Morgan, Edmund, 10
Moultrie, William, 75
Mulligan, Hercules, 78

N
Native Americans
  alliances of, 11, 63
  attacks by Pontiac, 15
  contact with colonists restricted, 13
  France and, 11
naval warfare, 70, 84, 86–88
Navigation Acts (1651, 1660, 1663, 1673), 10
Netherlands, 33, 88
New Jersey, 26, 57, 59–60, 63, 71
New York City, 20, 57–58, 61, 72, 77, 82, 86, 88
North, Lord Frederick, 25–26, 30, 32, 41, 89
Nova Scotia, Canada, 17, 57

O
O'Hara, Charles, 85
Old North Church, Boston, 43
Old South Meeting House, 36
Olive Branch Petition, 51–52
Oliver, Andrew, 21
Otis, James, Jr., 26

P
Paine, Thomas, 54, 56, 59, 67
Parker, John, 44
Patriot, The (movie), 81
peace treaty, 88
Pennsylvania, 26, 39–40, 48–49, 59, 62–65
Percy, General Hugh, 46
Perret, Geoffrey, 87
Philadelphia, Pennsylvania, 36, 39–40, 49, 51, 53, 56, 62–63, 65, 71, 77
Pitcairn, John, 44–46
Pontiac, 15
Prescott, Samuel, 43–44
Preston, Thomas, 32–34
Princeton, Battle of, 60
Proclamation of 1763, 13–15
Prohibitory Act (1776), 53
Pulaski, Casimir, 68

Q
Quartering Act (1765), 19, 38
Quebec, Canada, 51–53

R
racism
  against black British troops, 29–30
  against Native Americans, 15, 63
radical movement
  Loyal Nine and, 18
  Samuel Adams and, 17–18, 26, 35
  Sons of Liberty and, 18, 21, 23, 26, 30, 35–37
Regulars, 27, 29–30, 41, 43–45, 68, 71, 76, 78–79
religion, 58
Revenue Act
  colonial resistance, 26, 30
  passage of, 24–25
  repeal of, 30, 34
Revere, Paul, 28, 31, 33, 41–43
Rodrigue Hortalez et Compagnie, 53, 69
Rotch, Francis, 37
Royster, Charles, 67

Index **101**

rum, 16

S
Saratoga, Battle of, 65–69
Savannah, Georgia, 72
Scotland, 39, 70
Second Continental Congress, 48–53, 56–57, 63, 71
Serapis (ship), 70
Seven Years' War, 13, 53
Shays, Daniel, 90
Shays's Rebellion, 90
Shelburne, earl of, 88
Sherman, Roger, 56
Shy, John, 86
slave trade, 16, 30
Smith, Francis, 44–46
smuggling
    as colonial practice, 15–16
    cost to Britain of, 10
    Hancock and, 27
Sons of Liberty, 18, 21, 23, 26, 30, 35–37
South Carolina, 71–75, 78–79, 81
Spain, 11, 86–88
Stamp Act (1765), 18–21, 23–25
Stamp Act Congress, 19–20
Steuben, Baron Friedrich Wilhelm von, 65, 68
Sugar Act (1764), 17–18
Sumter, Thomas, 79
Supreme Court, 90
Swamp Fox, the, 79, 81

T
Tarleton, Lieutenant Colonel Banastre, 74–75, 77–79
taxation
    British need for, 10–11, 15
    under Confederation, 90
    enforcement by royal navy, 17, 37
    internal vs. external, 26
    molasses, 15–16
    representation and, 20, 25
    stamps, 18–19
    tea, 33–38

Tea Act (1773), 34–38
Townshend, Charles, 24–25
trade
    Boston harbor closed, 38
    boycotts of British goods, 21, 30, 40
    East India Company and, 34–35
    with France, 69
    importance to Great Britain of, 8, 10
    with Native Americans, 15
    restriction, 10, 15
    in slaves, 16, 30
    in sugar, molasses and rum, 16
    in tea, 34–35
    triangular, 16
Treaty of Alliance, 69
Treaty of Amity and Commerce, 69
Treaty of Paris (1763), 13
Treaty of Paris (1783), 88–89
Trenton, New Jersey, 59–60
triangular trade, 16

V
Valley Forge, Pennsylvania, 64–65, 68, 71
Virginia
    closing of port of Boston and, 38
    independence and, 56
    Stamp Act and, 19–20
    troops, 75–76

W
warships, 27–28, 59, 69, 72, 77, 84
Washington, George
    Arnold treason and, 77
    assault on Trenton, 59–60
    Battle of Bunker Hill and, 51
    chosen commander of Continental army, 49
    on Confederation, 90
    elected president, 92
    at First Continental Congress, 39–40
    Long Island, Battle of, 56–59
    Philadelphia and, 63–65
    Yorktown, 82, 84–85
Watson-Wentworth, Charles, Marquis of Rockingham, 23
Waxhaw Massacre, 75
West Indies, 10, 15–16, 87
West Point, 76–77
world war, 69

Y
Yorktown, Virginia, 80, 82–86

Picture Credits

Cover, pp. 9, 46 Bettmann/Getty Images; pp. 4–5 Kisialiou Yury/Shutterstock.com; p. 6 (top left), p. 7 (top), pp. 27, 31, 64 Courtesy of the Library of Congress; p. 6 (top right), p. 49 Everett - Art/Shutterstock.com; p. 6 (bottom), pp. 17, 83 Everett Historical/Shutterstock.com; p. 7 (bottom) Transcendental Graphics/Archive Photos/Getty Images; pp. 11, 22, 47, 80, 81 MPI/Stringer/Archive Photos/Getty Images; p. 14 Interim Archives/Archive Photos/Getty Images; p. 19 The New York Historical Society/Archive Photos/Getty Images; p. 20 Time & Life Pictures/The LIFE Picture Collection/Getty Images; p. 28 Kevin Myers/Wikimedia Commons; p. 29 Popperfoto/Getty Images; pp. 37, 42, 70 Ed Vebell/Archive Photos/Getty Images; p. 40 Archive Photos/Stringer/Archive Photos/Getty Images; p. 44 jejim/iStock/Thinkstock; pp. 50, 74 Buyenlarge/Archive Photos/Getty Images; p. 52 Print Collector/Hulton Fine Art Collection/Getty Images; pp. 55, 91 Courtesy of the National Archives; pp. 57, 66 Universal History Archive/Universal Images Group/Getty Images; p. 60 Time Life Pictures/The LIFE Picture Collection/Getty Images; p. 62 Searobin/Wikimedia Commons; p. 68 Kean Collection/Archive Photos/Getty Images; p. 76 Stock Montage/Archive Photos/Getty Images; p. 87 Print Collector/Hulton Archive/Getty Images; p. 89 Diego pmc/Wikimedia Commons.

About the Author

Amy B. Rogers is an experienced nonfiction author who has written many books for young readers on topics that include American history, science, and women's participation in sports. She lives in a suburb of Buffalo, New York, with her husband, Steve, and their Welsh corgi, Jiminy.